SAFFRON

Edible

Series Editor: Andrew F. Smith

EDIBLE is a revolutionary series of books dedicated to food and drink that explores the rich history of cuisine. Each book reveals the global history and culture of one type of food or beverage.

Already published

Apple Erika Janik, *Avocado* Jeff Miller, *Banana* Lorna Piatti-Farnell, *Barbecue* Jonathan Deutsch and Megan J. Elias, *Beans* Nathalie Rachel Morris, *Beef* Lorna Piatti-Farnell, *Beer* Gavin D. Smith, *Berries* Heather Arndt Anderson, *Biscuits and Cookies* Anastasia Edwards, *Brandy* Becky Sue Epstein, *Bread* William Rubel, *Cabbage* Meg Muckenhoupt, *Cake* Nicola Humble, *Caviar* Nichola Fletcher, *Champagne* Becky Sue Epstein, *Cheese* Andrew Dalby, *Chillies* Heather Arndt Anderson, *Chocolate* Sarah Moss and Alexander Badenoch, *Cocktails* Joseph M. Carlin, *Coffee* Jonathan Morris, *Corn* Michael Owen Jones, *Curry* Colleen Taylor Sen, *Dates* Nawal Nasrallah, *Doughnut* Heather Delancey Hunwick, *Dumplings* Barbara Gallani, *Edible Flowers* Constance L. Kirker and Mary Newman, *Eggs* Diane Toops, *Fats* Michelle Phillipov, *Figs* David C. Sutton, *Game* Paula Young Lee, *Gin* Lesley Jacobs Solmonson, *Hamburger* Andrew F. Smith, *Herbs* Gary Allen, *Herring* Kathy Hunt, *Honey* Lucy M. Long, *Hot Dog* Bruce Kraig, *Ice Cream* Laura B. Weiss, *Lamb* Brian Yarvin, *Lemon* Toby Sonneman, *Lobster* Elisabeth Townsend, *Melon* Sylvia Lovegren, *Milk* Hannah Velten, *Moonshine* Kevin R. Kosar, *Mushroom* Cynthia D. Bertelsen, *Mustard* Demet Güzey, *Nuts* Ken Albala, *Offal* Nina Edwards, *Olive* Fabrizia Lanza, *Onions and Garlic* Martha Jay, *Oranges* Clarissa Hyman, *Oyster* Carolyn Tillie, *Pancake* Ken Albala, *Pasta and Noodles* Kantha Shelke, *Pickles* Jan Davison, *Pie* Janet Clarkson, *Pineapple* Kaori O'Connor, *Pizza* Carol Helstosky, *Pomegranate* Damien Stone, *Pork* Katharine M. Rogers, *Potato* Andrew F. Smith, *Pudding* Jeri Quinzio, *Rice* Renee Marton, *Rum* Richard Foss, *Saffron* Ramin Ganeshram, *Salad* Judith Weinraub, *Salmon* Nicolaas Mink, *Sandwich* Bee Wilson, *Sauces* Maryann Tebben, *Sausage* Gary Allen, *Seaweed* Kaori O'Connor, *Shrimp* Yvette Florio Lane, *Soup* Janet Clarkson, *Spices* Fred Czarra, *Sugar* Andrew F. Smith, *Sweets and Candy* Laura Mason, *Tea* Helen Saberi, *Tequila* Ian Williams, *Tomato* Clarissa Hyman, *Truffle* Zachary Nowak, *Vanilla* Rosa Abreu-Runkel, *Vodka* Patricia Herlihy, *Water* Ian Miller, *Whiskey* Kevin R. Kosar, *Wine* Marc Millon

Saffron

A Global History

Ramin Ganeshram

REAKTION BOOKS

In memory of my mother

Published by Reaktion Books Ltd
Unit 32, Waterside
44–48 Wharf Road
London N1 7UX, UK
www.reaktionbooks.co.uk

First published 2020
Copyright © Ramin Ganeshram 2020

Printed and bound in India by Replika Press Pvt. Ltd

A catalogue record for this book is available from the British Library

ISBN 978 1 78914 330 0

Contents

Introduction

> Thy plants are an orchard of pomegranates with pleasant
> fruits; camphire, with spikenard. Spikenard and saffron,
> calamus and cinnamon . . .
> Song of Solomon (4:13–14)

Saffron – the thin, thread-like stigma of the autumn crocus (*Crocus sativus*) – is the world's most expensive and, some say, prized ingredient. Delicate in flavour with a unique aroma that some liken to fresh hay and others consider sharper and more astringent to the nose, saffron adds unique taste and colour to dishes. Sadly, modern cooks without a cultural association with saffron often steer clear of the spice, put off both by its cost and by an imperfect understanding of its value as a flavouring and colourant.

Whether saffron is a herb or a spice remains a topic of debate among scholars and culinarians, perhaps because its uses are so broad and span every course of cuisine. It may be that more than any other food product, saffron has consistently maintained an elevated worth over the many millennia that it has been harvested, never losing its value as culinary gold and forever entrenching itself in the human imagination.

NAMES.

SAFFRON.

PARTS USED.

only the Style
or Pistil.

A. زعفران
G. Kροx⊙.
L. Crocus.
I. Zaffrano.
G. Saffran.
F. Safran.
S. Aczafran.
D. Tamue·
·Saffwan.

PREPARATIONS.

A Tincture. A
Spirit. A Syrup.
an Extract.
and Plaister
or Oxycro-
cum.

PLACE.

Cambridgeshire
and Essex.

TIME.

Blossoms in
Sept.r or Oct.r

DESCRIPTION

The Root is a Solid Bulb.1. coverd with many thin coats of a fine Thready matter. and compressed top and Bottom. The Fibres 2. Grow round the bottom of the Root, long, and white as the Root. The Flower rises from the Centre of the Root 3, incompassed with Leaves, inclosed in a Whitish Skin. 4. The Leaves 5. are long, Narrow, of a deep Green, smooth, with a white Rib in the Middle, from the Centre of the Leaves en closed in a white film rises the flower 6, having Six Leaves of a very light purple at the upper Edges Strip'd, which nearer the Stalk becomes a Deep Rich Shining purple. The Three Styles 7. are red like Velvet open and Jagg'd at the Top but uniting in the Stalk lose their co lour and become a Transparent white. The Chives 8. are white at the Bottom becoming purple where they join the Apices 9. which are white. coverd with a Gold Coloured Farina 10. magnified—a leaf cut Transversely.

VIRTUES

Saffron is a high Cordial.

T. Sheldrake delin.

C.H. Hemerich sculp.

Saffron crocus (*Crocus sativus L.*): flowering stem with separate floral segments and corm and a description of the plant and its uses. Coloured line engraving by C. H. Hemerich, *c.* 1759, after Timothy Sheldrake.

The high cost of saffron arises largely from the fact that it requires harvesting by hand in precisely the right climate conditions. In developed nations, women and children are most often the harvesters of saffron, not only because their labour is the cheapest, but because the precision needed to pluck an intact crocus stigma from the flower is an act suited to smaller hands.

This labour-intensive crop was first harvested as a wild-flower in ancient Greece and has travelled worldwide both as a finished product and as a cultivar. Today, changing climate conditions are opening up new potential environments for the mass production of saffron beyond the Mediterranean and Middle Eastern locales where it is most often grown.

The preciousness of saffron has made it an attractive ingredient for different activities and industries, such as art, medicine, cosmetics and cloth-dyeing. Saffron traces can be found in cave art in Mesopotamia dating back at least 50,000 years, in the wall frescoes of ancient Santorini, in the dyed wrappings of Egyptian mummies and in the saffron-hued robes of Buddhist monks, but its main use has always been culinary. Saffron's high cost has made it the subject of trade wars throughout history, as well as smuggling schemes.

The importance of saffron was made clear to me as a child. In my parents' household, saffron was integral to our native cuisine but often as elusive as a unicorn. I grew up in New York City in the 1970s and '80s, when it was still difficult to obtain all the ingredients one needed to make every dish of my mother's Persian heritage – and saffron is an essential ingredient in Iranian cuisine.

I would go with my mother to Sahadi's and other Middle Eastern markets on Atlantic Avenue in Brooklyn to get most of the things she needed to prepare her cuisine. But her ever-hopeful enquiries about *zereshk* (barberries), *sohan*

Steamed, layered Persian rice, coloured with saffron.

(a caramelized sugar and nut brittle redolent with saffron) or *bastani* (saffron-flavoured Persian ice cream) were always met with regretful apologies from the shopkeepers along the Avenue.

Interestingly, one thing my mother never asked for was saffron itself. The saffron I knew arrived from Iran, along with the elusive barberries and various Persian sweets. It was packaged then, as it still is, in small, flat, round containers, and labelled with writing I couldn't understand. Whether my mother never purchased saffron in America because it was simply too expensive or because she believed that only Iranian saffron, right from the source, was worth the investment, I couldn't say, but many of my relatives today certainly express that sentiment.

As an adult and culinary historian, I often wonder if my mother simply considered the saffron sold in America not to be pure enough, regardless of its source. True saffron aficionados know only too well that saffron, like many other costly and rare ingredients, is often counterfeit.

Regardless of the reason, saffron was used sparingly in our household. Indeed, I am not even sure where my mother kept it, but it was certainly not with the other spices in the cabinet. My mother passed away when I was a young adult, and it was my cousin Shahnaz who taught me how to use a dry frying pan to toast the saffron in such a way that it was brittle enough to grind properly. Another relative showed me her trick of steeping the ground saffron in boiling water with a touch of sugar added as a preservative. This concoction could remain in the refrigerator ready for whenever it was needed. This same relative used, to my mind, a scandalous amount of saffron in her dishes, adding it as regularly as salt,

Bastani, Persian ice cream flavoured with saffron and pistachios.

pepper and the turmeric so common in Persian cuisine. It was hard to comprehend such hedonism.

My understanding of the preciousness of saffron was not related to the fact that it is the world's most expensive spice (its price, at times in its history, has approached that of gold). Certainly I was aware of this fact, but it meant little because, apart from other Iranians, I didn't know anyone who even used saffron, and so its value on the open market was an abstract concept to me.

Toast saffron in a small, dry frying pan over medium low heat to dry it out before grinding, if necessary.

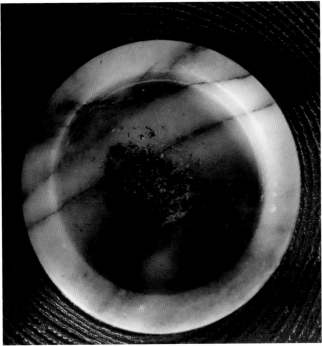

Adding a few grains of sugar can aid the grinding process to help ensure a finer powder.

Rather, to my mind, saffron was precious because it came from a homeland that had been closed off to us as a result of revolution and political strife. In that sense, it took on an almost-mythical characteristic – the source of an elixir that could transport one to deeply rooted ancestral histories. It was the scent of celebrations like *Nowruz*, the Persian New Year, when Iranian dishes, savoury and sweet but all redolent with saffron, loaded the table. It was the scent of sorrow, as my mother mixed a deeply hued and intense saffron water into halva, a dessert made out of toasted flour for mourning ceremonies.

Sohan-e qom, a brittle, heavily flavoured toffee with saffron, is an Iranian speciality.

While I had little knowledge of Western uses for saffron before I became a cook in adulthood and, later, a trained chef, there were always aspects of Western beliefs around saffron of which I was aware – notably that it was only useful for colour and that it had virtually no flavour or aroma. Those who use saffron often and appreciate its myriad qualities know that nothing could be further from the truth. Of course, the stunning colour imparted by saffron is its key feature, but its indescribable, almost astringent, aroma and flavour lends a delicate but unmistakable taste to dishes across many different canons of cuisine.

This book will give a comprehensive view of the history of saffron and the paths it has taken to become an internationally valued spice, as well as usage tips and recipes. As a start, in order to truly understand the value of saffron as a superior ingredient, most often used to elevate dishes to a certain level, one has to understand its route from humble Mediterranean origins through the Middle East and South Asia into Europe and through transatlantic trade beginning in the sixteenth century to the Caribbean and America.

This route was never a straight path with a clear trajectory. Rather, saffron was often introduced and reintroduced to various regions, traversing the same ground twice or three times. While, for example, wild saffron originated in Greece, it returned as a cultivar in the saddlebags of Alexander the Great's army. Prior to that, it had travelled from Assyria to Iran and then back again, as Persian conquerors attempted to rebuild their famed gardens in the lands they overtook. This book will follow saffron's circuitous routes and explore how, over the centuries, like other precious commodities, saffron has experienced its share of black-market sales and even counterfeiting by unscrupulous traders looking to cash in on this floral gold.

In these pages, saffron's value as a medicinal ingredient will be examined, from antiquity, when its uses are noted in

Unlike Levantine halva, Persian halva is a thick paste made from flour, butter and saffron.

Arancini are balls made from saffron risotto that are rolled in breadcrumbs before deep frying.

the texts of the Persian physician Ibn Sina (Avicenna) and the Roman physician Galen, on to the Middle Ages. Today, much of this ancient research is being re-examined by scientists and healthcare practitioners. It should be noted that references to historical directions and modern research about saffron's use as a medicinal agent are for historical or informational purposes only and should not be considered as medical advice.

The book will also cover lesser-known saffron culture, such as that of the communities of German immigrants who arrived in Lancaster County, Pennsylvania, in the early eighteenth century and were so well known for their prodigious use of saffron that they became known as the 'Yellow Dutch' (a misunderstanding of the word *Deutsch*).

Finally, a recipe section at the end endeavours to share classic recipes from various cultures that use saffron, as well some that are newer and more innovative.

I

Flower of the Gods: Origin and Early Cultivation

As Dawn prepared to spread her saffron mantle over the land,
Zeus the Thunderer gathered the gods to the highest peak of
many-ridged Olympus, and spoke to them while all listened.

Homer, *The Iliad*

Among the stories of metamorphoses so integral to Greek
mythology is the tale of Crocus and Smilax. Crocus, a hand-
some youth, falls in love with the woodland nymph Smilax
and pursues her relentlessly. Eventually, the gods tire of their
overzealous passion and turn them into the plants that bear
their names – Crocus (saffron) and Smilax (greenbrier, or
yew) respectively: 'The loves, then, of Crocus, and of Smilax,
who were both turned into flowers, not being able to enjoy
themselves together.'[1]

At first blush, the delicate little bloom that is the crocus
hardly seems a worthy exemplar of the obsessive passion of a
pair of virile young lovers, but closer examination proves that
assumption wrong. The most valued parts of the flower – that
which ultimately becomes the saffron thread – are the long,
thin stigmas protruding from its centre, waiting to be plucked
and dried. These stigmas are nothing more than the exagger-
ated sexual organs of the plant. Ironically, saffron is a sterile

Nicolas Poussin, *Realm of Flora*, 1631, oil on canvas, detail of Crocus and Smilax, whose overzealous love led them to be metamorphosed into the plants that bear their names.

male species that reproduces itself through the generation of daughter 'corms' – small bulb-like extensions from which the crocus emerges.

While both corms and bulbs are the base of what are called 'vascular' plants, when it comes to corms, 'bulb-*like*' is the operative term. While often confused with true bulbs, such as those of lilies or tulips, corms are a very different entity. Corms are essentially an extension of the plant stem that, if cut open, appear to be solid. Conversely, a bulb has layers – think of an onion.

A bulb essentially provides a food source for the plant, which goes through a flowering (reproductive) cycle and a vegetative cycle. Bulbs have five parts: a basal plate from which the roots grow; layers, or 'scales', where nutrients for the plant are stored; a thin papery layer called the 'tunic', which covers the scales; an embryo for the flower; and lateral buds which will eventually spread out and enlarge into their own bulbs. Bulbs benefit from being separated over time so they have more room to spread out and reproduce.

Corms work in a similar way to bulbs in that the corm itself is covered with a thin paper-like membrane that protects it from weevils and other underground pests. Baby corms, called cormels, will form at the base of the mother corm and eventually grow on their own, along with root-like structures called stolons. The stolons form at the tips of the cormels and allow them to penetrate more deeply into the soil if the nutritive conditions warrant it. As the cormels grow into flowers, the mother corm is used up for nutrition and eventually shrivels to nothing.

Stages of saffron, from left to right: a saffron crocus petal; young shoots with the crocus flower emerging; semi-mature crocus flower; picked immature flower; almost mature flower; mature flower with almost developed stigmas; fully mature flower with developed stigmas; picked stigmas with discarded petals; finally, a pile of picked stigmas, ready for drying.

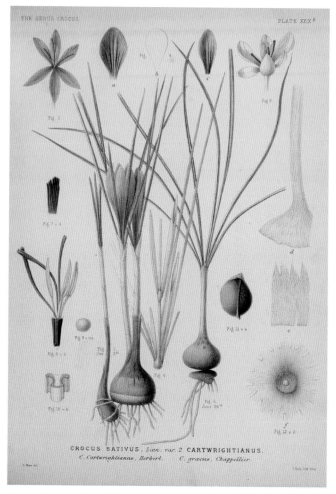

George Maw's coloured line engraving of the original wild saffron, *Crocus cartwrightianus*, in *A Monograph of the Genus Crocus* (1886). This demonstrates the reproductive parts of the plant.

The saffron crocus (*Crocus sativus*) bears a close resemblance to the common spring crocus (*Crocus vernus*), which is also a corm-based plant, but saffron croci bloom in the autumn to early winter, emerging to fullness in late September to early October, with a growing season that can extend into November.

The earliest saffron was a wild species that scientists in Germany have recently confirmed originated in Greece, near Athens.[2] This variety, *Crocus cartwrightianus*, was the precursor to *Crocus sativus* and the corms of the plants with the longest and most robust stigmas were selected for domestication, thereby creating a selection process for a plant that is otherwise immune to hybridization.

Saffron's original homeland enjoyed, on average, 500 mm (20 in.) of rainfall per year, which is markedly different from that of the regions to which it ultimately spread. The saffron crocus grows best in high-altitude regions with arid climates and relatively poor soil conditions. In some ways, like fine wine grapes, the saffron crocus must 'suffer' to produce the best-quality end product.

For some time, the Greek island of Santorini, known to the Minoan civilization as Thera, was considered to be the original source of wild saffron because of a series of wall frescoes unearthed there in the Akrotiri settlement. Encapsulated and preserved in volcanic lava and ash from a late Bronze Age volcanic eruption on the island, the wall paintings depict women and monkeys picking saffron under the guidance of a goddess.

Texts and archaeological evidence from Akrotiri indicate that saffron was used heavily in perfumes and for medicinal purposes, notably those for women and girls (including gynaecological uses). One wall painting specifically depicts a woman treating the wounded foot of a girl with saffron.

At the ruins of Akrotiri, wall paintings depicting the importance of saffron abound.

Scholars have speculated that the representations of saffron as most related to women in this Bronze Age society might mean that women were the primary tenders of the plant and claimed the majority of knowledge and utilization of its prized stigmas.

The attention given to the crocus in these paintings, and the presence of a goddess (the gods were considered responsible for the provision of medicine and physic in Minoan culture), indicates its value for religious and medicinal purposes. In common life, saffron was used to dye the distinctive, short bolero-type jackets worn by Minoan women and depicted in wall frescoes and on urns. Saffron was also used in women's cosmetics.

Yet, despite its clearly prominent place in this culture, saffron wasn't actively cultivated in Greece or Thera. In keeping with the Minoans' nature-based civilization, the gift of saffron was left, instead, to the caprice of the natural world, ruled by a pantheon of gods. As such, saffron was a foraged crop that rewarded those who sought its golden threads in a limited manner, based on the whims of environment and season. This only enhanced its rarity and value.

On other Greek islands and in Egypt, saffron features in frescoes not unlike those in Thera, seeming to imply trade of saffron between the regions, especially given the presence of Egyptian-origin goods on the walls of the Akrotiri

A woman gathers saffron in this 3,600-year-old wall painting in the ancient Theran city of Akrotiri, Santorini.

Jalebi, also called zouloubia, is common in South Asia, the Middle East and Indian diasporic communities.

settlement, including ostrich eggs and ivory. Saffron also appears in the Hebrew *Song of Solomon* a full thousand years before Minoan civilization reached its peak, indicating that the ancient Hebrews had access to saffron through trade as well.

Saffron is likely to have come to the Hebrews via Phoenician traders. Phoenicians were Semitic tribal people who originated in the Levant, centred mainly around modern Lebanon.

Saffron's reach as a wild harvest traded on the open market of the ancient world is impressive, but it was the Persians who first cultivated saffron as a staple crop as early as the tenth century BCE, the corms having made their way east – again, most likely in the pouches of Phoenician traders.

The Persians quickly learned from its first inception as a harvested crop that saffron is famously fickle. It does best in well-drained, loose soil. Corms are planted two or three together, and roughly 10 to 15 cm (4 to 6 in.) apart, in furrows with 2 to 3 cm (around an inch) of space between each corm. Precise planting configurations differ slightly in saffron-growing regions, from the Mediterranean to South Asia to North America. The Persians grew the crocus in long, even rows, raked out of arid soil, turning fields of near-colourless dirt into a boundless haze of purple when in bloom. Even in antiquity, visitors to Persia noted the vast fields of saffron that reached far into land otherwise largely inhospitable to agriculture.

The methods Persians learned for propagating and harvesting saffron remain the same today. Regardless of where saffron is grown, ample space is necessary so that the main 'mother' corms can reproduce smaller 'daughter' cormels. This produces thickly populated beds over time, which have to be dug up, separated and replanted. In some climates, the corms are wintered over out of the ground and replanted in late spring to early summer for an autumn harvest. Separating daughter corms from the mother can be a tricky business: not all cormels survive being pulled off the main corm and many growers prefer to leave the plant undisturbed, allowing it to grow in thickly thatched beds, as long as the closeness of the blooms does not make harvesting the stigmas too difficult.

Once the crocus flower emerges in the autumn, the real work begins. As a hand-harvested crop, saffron is not only laborious to cultivate but highly perishable, with a short window of time in which to pick. Harvest must take place in the morning after the dew has evaporated but before the flowers begin to shrivel in the sun. This means that saffron pickers need to work fast at the back-breaking task of bending over to pluck the flower heads from the stalks.

Removing the stigmas from the flower must be done quickly as well, since the flower begins to wither very quickly after harvest. The stigmas are laid out and covered with a thin piece of gauze or cloth in a dry place. Modern mass-producers use low-temperature dryers to dry out the stigmas quickly and evenly.

The number of flowers needed to produce 1 kg (2.2 lb) of finished saffron varies, based on growing region and condition, between 70,000 and 200,000 flowers. For example, according to John Timbs's book *Things Not Generally Known, Familiarly Explained: A Book for Old and Young* (1866), the croci grown in Essex, England, required 40,000 flowers to produce 0.45 kg (1 lb) of saffron.[3] Timbs goes on to write, 'The old statement that 203,920 flowers are requisite is a gross exaggeration.' One wonders where such a precise number came from.

The low yield from each flower – up to three thread-like stigmas each – requires extensive acreage to produce any significant yield. Moreover, the extreme amount of work needed

The saffron crocus grows from corms, often mistaken for bulbs.

A saffron gatherer in Afghanistan.

to produce saffron necessitates that it be produced in regions with a cheaply available labour force. In areas like Afghanistan, Iran and Kashmir in India, inexpensive labourers most often tend to be women and children.

John Spurrier, an English farmer in Delaware, described the process of harvesting saffron as follows, in his book *The Practical Farmer* of 1793:

> The most proper time for this is early in the morning, when the whole flowers are to be gathered, and thrown handful by handful into a basket; having then carried home all you have got, immediately spread them upon a large table, and fall to picking out the filamenta stylis, or chives and together with them a pretty long proportion

of the stylus itself, or string to which they are joined; the rest of the flower may be thrown away as useless.[4]

In the Middle East, the 'useless' flowers are generally used to feed livestock.

The most prolific New World growers of saffron were the Schwenkfelders, a religious group, later Mennonites, who carried saffron corms with them from Germany, where they were known for its cultivation. Martin Keen is a descendant of the original Mennonites who settled in Lancaster County. He has a food science background and spent more than a decade growing and selling saffron as a way to diversify the crops on his small family farm. Keen had been familiar with saffron in the home gardens and recipes of his mother and grandmother.

Over the course of his long career, Keen has seen farmers and would-be home cultivators lured into growing saffron by the excessively high price commanded by the spice, which can range from hundreds to thousands of dollars per pound, depending on its origin and grade. They see an exorbitantly priced cash crop, with a higher payout than any other – but, he says, they are not fully aware of how much hand labour goes into producing it.

> If you pick for an hour, it takes three times as long to pluck out the stigmas and you have to work as fast as you can. If you are picking a lot you are only sleeping two to three hours a night to get it all out. I've always said that harvesting saffron takes a strong back and weak mind. That's why it moves to wherever labour is cheapest.

According to current estimates, four hundred hours of labour are needed to produce 1 kg (2.2 lb) of saffron.[5]

The high-touch production of saffron makes it the ultimate artisanal crop, requiring nurture and skill by those who produce it. Consumers pay for that dedication at the market. But despite the steep price of saffron, Keen insists, consumers are getting great value for their dollar.

> The truth is that, in the end, you aren't paying that much based on labour. What you are paying is about seven cents per flower – try and go into a florist and buy any decorative flower – they are all produced with a lot less work and cost a lot more than seven cents. Saffron appears to be high cost for its weight but the amount of labour is phenomenal. In a way you are getting a deal given the labour that goes into it.[6]

2

The Ancient World and the Silk Road

[Of] this wily race be wary, for saffron was stirred
into their dishes for no other reason than to befuddle
and weaken the brain.
Ancient warning for travellers to Persia[1]

It was those skilled sailors from the Levant, the Phoenicians, who brought saffron both in processed form and its corms to their homeland, but also through trade to Egypt, Iran (Persia) and the Roman Empire.

Of these, it was the Persians who became most enamoured of the golden filaments that were being obtained through trade. In what could only be called a growing obsession, early Iranians found ingenious ways to incorporate saffron into everything from household goods to cosmetics to medicine to food.

As early as the tenth century BCE, early versions of the rugs for which Persian weavers became so famous for millennia after featured saffron threads within the weave. Later, the intense yellow colour that could be extracted from the stigmas became a key dye in these floor coverings that featured elaborate garden designs. Even in death, the Iranians kept their saffron close, using it to dye burial shrouds, just as the

Mîrzâ Bâqir,
*Saffron (Crocus
sativus), al-za'furân,*
fol. 29, 1889–90.

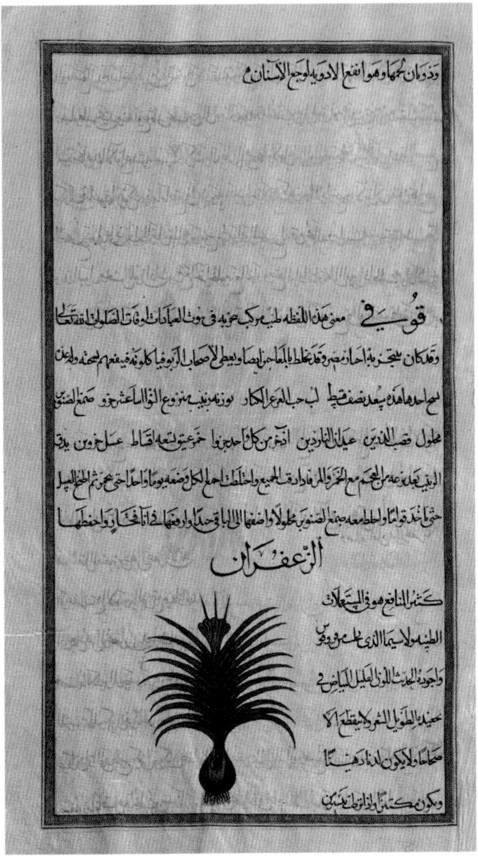

Egyptians used it to dye the wrappings of noble mummies. Persians also used saffron in bathing water, considering its astringent and clean-smelling scent a cleansing agent, and also a medication to soothe bruised or ruptured skin. The Persians' most triumphant use of the precious spice, however, was culinary.

Known for their elaborately elegant mode of eating in antiquity, as they are in modern times, Persians based cuisine

Phoenicians plied a successful trade route via water and brought saffron from Greece to Egypt and the Middle East, where it was cultivated. From *The Illustrated History of the World for the English People*, vol. 1 (1881).

on the principle of *sarde o garme*, or 'cold and hot', properties of their food in a methodology very similar to Indian Ayurveda. Hot foods were not necessarily spicy or warm in temperature, just as cold foods were not necessarily chilled, temperature-wise. Rather, this principle was based on inherent properties of foods and how they allegedly operated within the body metabolically, ultimately affecting everything from disease to demeanour. If, for example, people were suffering from ailments that were thought to be provoked by hot foods – say, a skin eruption or rash – they were given cold foods as an antidote.

Persian cooks strove then, as now, to balance hot and cold foods in every culinary preparation. Saffron, which was considered hot by nature, was used to flavour stews, desserts, teas and tisanes. Most notably, the spice was integral to the layered rice dishes called *polow*, for which the Persians were most esteemed and upon which Mogul Indian biryani and later pilafs are based. Rice, which is integral to Persian cuisine, is considered a 'cold' food, so its pairing with saffron was both logical and desirable.

Given this prodigious use of saffron, Persians did not long remain satisfied with the limited access to the spice afforded by the trade routes, and by the tenth century BCE saffron was being formally cultivated in orderly rows over vast tracts of land in Iran.

As much as Greece was the original source of saffron itself, Iran was the source of its true international reach. After that initial journey in the pouches and pockets of Phoenician traders, it was the Iranians who brought the love of saffron to the world using the Royal Road, which traversed much of what would become a vast empire, spanning, at its height, all of the Middle East to the Caucasus, to North Africa and the

Biryani is a layered rice dish featuring saffron that came to India through Iran at the time of the Mogul emperors.

border of Europe via Greece and Turkey. Potentially formed by earlier routes created by Assyrian kings, the Royal Road was a postal route that served as the original 'Pony Express', about which Herodotus wrote: 'Neither snow nor rain nor heat nor gloom of night stays these couriers from the swift completion of their appointed rounds.'[2]

There is every reason to believe that this ancient route was involved in the transport of saffron even before the rise of the Persian Empire in the Assyrian period, a pre-Iranian empire covering much of the known world. The empire then included latter-day Persia/Iran until just after its height in the seventh century BCE under the rule of King Ashur-banipal, when early Iranians revolted against their Assyrian overlords.

Ashurbanipal and his predecessors were known for their love of botany. Ancient texts of the time describe the attention

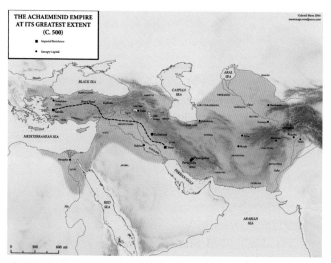

The Royal Road operated in the Persian Empire in the 5th century BCE under the rule of Darius the Great. Saffron likely travelled this route at the height of the empire.

34

Engraving of a sketch by James Ferguson, 'The Palaces of Nineveh Restored', from Sir Austen Henry Layard, *The Monuments of Nineveh* (1853).

they paid to their royal gardens, where exotic plants brought by trade and conquest were cultivated. Within these pleasure gardens, the saffron crocus enjoyed a place of prominence. Some scholars have speculated that King Ashurbanipal's gardens at the Assyrian capital Nineveh were the actual Hanging Gardens of Babylon referred to by Herodotus as one of the Seven Wonders of the Ancient World. An ancient botanical text said to have been written by Ashurbanipal outlines the uses of saffron as a medicinal plant. Elsewhere there is reference to the Neo-Assyrian city of Azupiranu, or 'Saffron City' – but it is not known whether the city was so called because saffron was cultivated there on a large scale or simply because the town was a key trading post for the spice.

Later the Persians, like the Assyrians before them (or perhaps even taking cues from their predecessors), became known for their lush, enclosed gardens, or *paradeisos* (the origin of the word 'paradise'), filled with fruit trees and rare botanicals, some for their beauty and many more for their culinary and medicinal purposes. Again, chief among these was the saffron crocus.

As the Persians pursued their course of empire building, they spread the saffron corm wherever they intended to spread the influence of Persian culture. Over a period of more than two and a half millennia, this reach extended to Kashmir on the Indian subcontinent, where cultivation of saffron was successful enough by the sixth century BCE for Kashmiri saffron to become a desirable commodity on the Phoenician trading routes. Consequently, it made its way back to Greece, not only as pure saffron but in the form of perfume and medicines. The climate of Kashmir produced an exceptionally aromatic and deeply coloured saffron thread that ultimately surpassed both Grecian and Persian saffron in value, even in those nations. Kashmiri saffron continues to be the most prized – and most expensive – today.

Persian rice pudding depends on saffron for colour and flavour.

The Macedonian prince Alexander the Great conquered the Persian empire in the 4th century BCE and adopted its customs, including the adoration of saffron. Detail from the *Battle of Issus*, *c.* 100 BCE, a Roman floor mosaic originally from the House of the Faun in Pompeii, now on display in the National Museum of Archaeology in Naples.

The Persian love of saffron was well entrenched by the time Alexander the Great pushed east into Iran on his mission of world conquest in the fourth century BCE. Certainly, the Macedonian prince had knowledge of saffron, but the Persian obsession with the spice must surely have been something of a surprise. Soon enough, however, he, too, quickly succumbed to its allure.

Of all the lands conquered by Alexander's army, none had the emotional sway upon the leader that Iran did, and he quickly adopted all manner of Persian customs. This included wearing Persian clothes and adopting the Iranians' form of religious worship; he also married Roxana, the daughter of the conquered Persian king Darius. But he embodied his adopted land most fully in his use of saffron, from consuming the layered rice dishes hued gold with saffron water to taking medicinal baths heavily steeped with saffron, said to be an effective remedy for soothing aching muscles and curing battle wounds. In fact, he believed this to be so therapeutic that he prescribed it as a course of treatment for all of his soldiers.

Alexander's belief in the therapeutic and cultural value of saffron was so great that his lavish use of the precious threads became an effective marketing ploy for traders who hawked saffron throughout the known world, but particularly back in the Mediterranean, where Alexander's conquest had already earned him god-like status. Claiming their wares to be the very variety used by Alexander, or touting the many benefits he had recognized in the spice, traders stirred up consumers' desire for saffron. In some ways, the Macedonian prince became saffron's celebrity spokesperson.

A century later Iran became a major centre for trading silk, operating as a bridge on the northern silk routes between China in the East, the Middle East and Europe beyond in the West. The exchange of goods was not one-way, nor was it

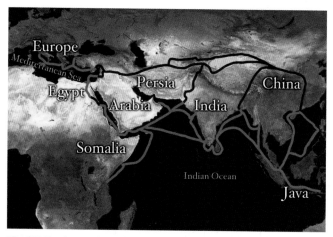

The Silk Road expanded saffron's reach even further than the original Persian Royal Road, enabling the spice to travel to India, China and Europe.

L NEST point eſtrange que ſe feu tom=
bant du cieſ bruſſe ſes ſieux qu'iſ attamēt
mais iſ eſt monſtrueux de ſe voir yſſir

Pliny the Elder wrote extensively about the propagation of saffron in his *Natural History*. Illustration from Pierre Boaistuau's 16th-century *Histoires prodigieuses*.

limited to silk. Dates, pistachios and saffron are recorded as entering China from Iran. In one third-century Chinese text, writer Wan Zhen makes note of the saffron being grown in Kashmir, where it was mixed with wine and its flowers given as a ritual offering to Buddha.[3] This indicates that saffron must have also entered China via a southerly silk route that traversed Kashmir.

Medieval Chinese texts indicate that saffron was not only used to scent wine. The spice took on a singular medicinal purpose, for which it is still used today. Saffron was believed to have the ability to ward off offensive smells and generally be a purifier for the body against bad *chi* – the 'vital energy' of any living thing. Perfumes were also made from saffron in China at this time. Interestingly, then as now, there was limited, if any, use of saffron in traditional Chinese cuisine.

It can be said that saffron was something of a soldier of fortune in an ancient world that saw empires rise and fall. With conquest and the forced and amiable interchange of cultural ideas, as well as the ever-expanding commercial enterprises that built trade on both land and water, saffron managed to remain consistently on the bill of saleable goods, either as a finished spice or in the form of corms for cultivation. This remained the case even as other exotics fell out of fashion or favour.

The Romans, who held sway over the last and largest European empire before the onset of the Dark Ages, were no less susceptible to the charms of the saffron crocus than other ancient cultures. Early Romans certainly encountered it first in trade with Minoans and then later through conquest. As Rome took over much of what is today Europe and parts of the Middle East and North Africa, it was ideally placed to bring saffron further west and throughout imperial Rome. The Romans' lavish use of saffron was a way to demonstrate the empire's mind-boggling wealth. Romans used saffron in their baths, as perfume and in extravagant dishes; it was even strewn along the streets to cleanse the air of the malodorous vapours of daily life.

3

Saffron in the Medieval and Renaissance Eras

Common or best-knowne Saffron growth plentifully
in Cambridge-shire, Saffron-Walden, and other places
thereabout, as corne in the field.
John Gerard, *The Herball; or, Generall Historie of Plantes* (1597)

The spread of saffron in Europe can be largely attributed to the spread of the Roman Empire, but when the empire collapsed in 476 CE, ushering in the Middle Ages, saffron production declined. It took another three hundred years before the Moors – Muslims from North Africa – brought saffron to Spain, where they had established hegemony in the Iberian peninsula that would last for eight hundred years.

During this period, considered the 'Dark Ages' throughout Europe, arts, culture and science in the Islamic empire flourished. With their arrival in Spain, the Muslim conquerors established irrigation systems that dramatically increased productivity of native produce but also allowed for the import and cultivation of the foods of their homelands – notably the saffron crocus. Areas like La Mancha became centres of saffron production, with fortunes being built upon its trade. Several family coats of arms and municipal crests from this area of Spain prominently feature the saffron crocus, and the

Spanish word for saffron, *azafrán*, comes from the Arabic word for the spice: *zafaran*. Both words are pronounced very much like 'saffron', with either a harder 'z' sound at the beginning of each and more pronounced 'ah' sounds in the middle, or with a 'th' sound.

The Moors' use of saffron was both culinary and medicinal. Evidence of their influence in Spain can be still be seen in saffron-infused paella, perhaps the most recognizable and traditional of Spanish dishes and one which bears a close resemblance to the layered rice dishes of the Middle East.

Spanish women picking saffron stigmas in the late 19th or early 20th century.

A traditional dish of Spain, paella probably evolved from *polow* and, later, the biryani of the Persian/Mogul world, then was adopted by Arab invaders who made their way to Spain.

Physicians throughout the medieval Islamic world were very clear on saffron use as a curative, often dedicating whole texts to the specifics of its medical properties. In the twelfth century, the Persian physician Ibn Sina (Avicenna) noted its usefulness in everything from diseases of the eye and liver to respiratory distress and gynaecological problems. Ibn Sina's Arabic contemporary Ibn Nafis Qarshi also recommended saffron as a cardiac tonic, to improve complexion and even as a hypnotic and cure for headache and melancholy. Even today, saffron pickers and packers often speak anecdotally about how saffron's heady aroma can induce a euphoric state, leading modern researchers to scientifically explore its well-documented historical use as an antidepressant.[1] In the Middle Ages, it was also universally known to be an astringent that was ideal for purifying ill-humoured organs, skin lesions and the like.[2]

While the Iberian Peninsula remained dedicated to the use of saffron, thanks to centuries of Muslim influence, the rest of Europe does not seem to have consistently continued its use until the Crusades brought Europeans back into the Middle East.

A military engagement waged by European Christians, eager to wrest the holy city of Jerusalem from Muslim control, the Crusades took place from the eleventh to the thirteenth centuries. Crusaders, mostly from France, Germany and England, spent months and sometimes years in the Muslim territories of the Middle East, entering through the Bosporus into the Byzantine Empire through Constantinople (later Istanbul). The Byzantine Empire had long controlled the major trade routes into the Far East and was a conduit for the import of saffron, which was used widely throughout the empire for medicine and perfumery. This love of saffron did not wane during the Middle Ages, even as Turkish Muslim invasions encroached closer and closer to Constantinople, making trade even more perilous. The Turks themselves had been well known in antiquity as growers and traders of the saffron crocus. The first-century Roman writer Columella wrote of the famed saffron of Corycus, a town in Cilicia – an area that correlates to Çukurova in modern-day Turkey:

> They say that Timolus and Corycus are considered famous for the saffron-flower, and Judaea and Arabia for their precious scents; but that our own community is not destitute of aforesaid plants, for in many sections of the city we see at one time cassia putting forth its leaves, again the frankincense plant, and gardens blooming with myrrh and saffron.[3]

Columella's 'own community' was the region of what is today Cádiz in Spain.

The extended time the Crusaders spent pushing forward through the Byzantine Empire towards Jerusalem must surely have reacquainted these Europeans with an array of exotic spices and foods to be had there, including saffron. The Crusaders reached Jerusalem in 1099, occupying the city for nearly a hundred years and then again for a brief twenty-year period in the thirteenth century.

An occupied city requires oversight by its conquerors, and Europeans, acting as administrators and soldiers, took up residence in Jerusalem. Many took Middle Eastern wives, who brought saffron-laden cooking into their homes, along with saffron perfumes and medicines. The interplay between the European expatriate community and the natives of the lands they had conquered naturally meant that the Europeans developed a taste for saffron, and they took the spice back to their homes in Europe, often using covert means: spiriting the cormels away in hidden compartments of containers, buried under other spices, or wrapped in rugs and other fabrics.

The resurgence in the European taste for saffron during this time is well documented. It reached its peak alongside the high point of the bubonic plague epidemic, for which saffron was widely believed to be an effective cure.

In terms of cuisine, we see saffron appear in recipes and shopping lists throughout medieval Western Europe. One medieval Flemish cookbook offers a recipe for a sauce to accompany rabbit, which includes cinnamon, saffron, ginger and sugar. A shopping list for a wedding feast outlined in the French cookbook *Le Ménagier de Paris*, penned in the late thirteenth century, included 'long pepper, galingale [galangal, which is similar to ginger]; cloves, saffron and other spices'.

The most reliable access to saffron for Europeans at this time was through Venice, which had long straddled the line between loyalty to Christianity and loyalty to commerce, and which was known internationally for the brutal lengths it would go to protect its lucrative business as middleman in the East–West spice trade. Venice was ideally situated on the Adriatic Sea, where it had obtained vast trading rights, and Venetians were eminently skilled as mariners to make the journey to Constantinople. This well-established trade route became one of the most prominent maritime silk routes and is now recognized by the United Nations Educational, Scientific and Cultural Organization (UNESCO).

When Venice, acting as an independent city-state, orchestrated the attack and pillage of Constantinople in 1204 under the Crusaders' flag, a door was opened to untold wealth via the spice trade. It was only a matter of time before the Venetians were trading on the silk routes into Persia and other outreaches of the Mongol Empire, which was spreading so fast that, by the end of the thirteenth century, it would cover most of the Middle East, all of China, Southeast Asia, parts of Russia and the northern outposts of the Indian subcontinent, most notably Kashmir. Trading with the Mongols meant trading with those who controlled the saffron market.

Some Crusaders brought back with them not just saffron but the corms required to grow it in their home countries. This was no small feat, because the punishments for taking saffron corms from Muslim trading areas were severe and often included death. Still, a number of efforts were clearly successful because a small but pervasive saffron-growing culture blossomed in Western Europe.

A notable example was in the English town of Saffron Walden, where legend has it that a thirteenth-century Christian pilgrim travelling to Jerusalem had managed to smuggle a single saffron corm in his staff and, upon his return to England, was able to propagate it in his Essex town. The town, originally know as Chepying (Market) Walden, was best known for its wool trade in the Middle Ages. However, by

Raphael Tuck & Sons, *The Old Houses, Saffron Walden*, *c.* 1906, postcard.

Ibn Butlan, 'Peasant Picking Saffron', from the medieval health handbook *Tacuinum sanitatis* (1380–99).

the 1500s the area was so well known for its prolific saffron production that it was renamed Saffron Walden.

Long after saffron cultivation ceased in Saffron Walden, the legend of how it came to be a saffron centre in England continued. John Timbs devotes two pages to saffron in his 1866 book *Things Not Generally Known*, and quotes English writer Richard Hakluyt, his predecessor by more than two hundred years, regarding the crocus and its arrival in Essex:

Hakluyt was told at Saffron Walden, that a pilgrim brought from the Levant to England, in the reign of Edward III, the first root of Saffron, which he had found means to conceal in his staff, made hollow for that purpose: 'and so', says Hakluyt, 'he brought this root into this realm with venture of his life; for if he had been taken, by the law of the country from whence it came, he had died for the fact.'[4]

When the bubonic plague, also known as the Black Death, roared through Europe in the fourteenth century, it sorely taxed the saffron supply, whether imported or grown locally in towns like Saffron Walden. This was in part because saffron was believed to be a cure for the plague and also because a good number of saffron farmers themselves died of the disease. There was no one to tend and harvest this labour-intensive crop – an irony that was apparently lost on those who believed in its curative properties.

This desperate scramble for saffron led once again to aggressive attempts to source the spice from the major producing areas, but, unfortunately for Europeans suffering from both plague and saffron fever, the supply of the precious stigmas from the crocus from Muslim nations was not forthcoming after the brutal East–West engagements during the Crusades. Even the Venetians' access had waned, and it was left to Greece to fulfil its ancient role as saffron provider to the world. Saffron prices skyrocketed because of the limited quantities the Venetians could reasonably secure, as well as the vast distances it had to travel to get to the markets of Europe. As always, the extensive labour required to harvest the precious spice drove the price up further, as it still does today.

A particularly notable example of this was the thirteenth-century Saffron War, in which a private merchant's consignment of 363 kg (800 lb) of saffron, valued anywhere from U.S.$300,000 to U.S.$500,000 in modern currency, was hijacked en route to Basel in Switzerland. Hostilities grew while the shipment was held hostage for fourteen weeks until it was eventually returned. This incident, while notable for the sheer value of the stolen shipment, was nothing out of the ordinary. Attacks on saffron-bearing ships were commonplace, with pirates even forgoing ships laden with gold to target Venetian and Genoan vessels working the saffron trade.

Concern about market limitations further encouraged local European growth of the saffron crocus. In Basel, a hard lesson having been learned, locals planted their own corms and had nearly a decade of lucrative success. Still, the crops had to be protected from thieves by armed guards, and harsh penalties were imposed for digging up the corms and for attempting to take them out of the town borders.

Austria, Germany, France, Greece and Italy followed England and Switzerland in saffron cultivation, but it was Nuremberg in Germany that truly became the European centre for the spice, as well as other imported commodities. The city's dominance in this area was largely because of a forward-thinking and advantageous series of trade agreements it made throughout Europe during the thirteenth and fourteenth centuries, which included tariff-reduction treaties, safe-passage accords and mutual trade agreements.[5]

Given Nuremberg's place of prominence as a mercantile centre, the city's leaders were not going to take hindrances to its business dealings lightly, particularly when it came to saffron, which was the most valuable of the commodities it traded. The counterfeiting of saffron had become a problem equal to piracy and smuggling, so, in the fifteenth century, in order to discourage the attempts of those who would ply false saffron, Nuremberg enacted a series of laws called the

Even in far northern Europe, saffron was purchased as a gourmet ingredient. It has long been featured in these Christmas buns from Scandinavia.

Safranschou. These outlined penalties for saffron counterfeiting. Depending on the severity of the crime, these punishments included fines, imprisonment and torture, and even execution by methods such as being buried alive.

These protections made saffron-trading Nuremberg families rich, including that of sixteenth-century Katerina Imhoff Lemmel, a businesswoman who worked in her family's saffron company prior to taking vows as a nun. Nuns at Lemmel's Birgittine convent, Maria Mai in Bavaria, were using saffron almost to excess as both a stimulant and a nervine. Lemmel's letters back home included purchase orders for up to 1 kg (just over 2 lb) of saffron a year to aid the fifty or sixty nuns in their tasks of singing and praying for most of their waking hours during Lent – acts, she wrote, that could only be made easier with saffron.[6]

Medieval nuns had a taste for saffron, which they believed would keep their spirits up through long days and nights of prayer. Illustration from *Arzneibuch* (Compendium of Popular Medicine and Surgery) of *c.* 1675.

Henry VIII, the sixteenth-century English Tudor monarch, found that he too had to protect his saffron supplies – not from counterfeiters, but from ladies who found they could not do without it. In this case, the monarch's female courtiers wanted to get their hands on the crocus stigmas in order to dye their hair. The king had to enact a ban to prevent the practice so that his precious saffron could be used for more important activities – culinary, medicinal and cloth-dyeing. His predecessor, Henry VII, banned the 'wild' Irish from using saffron to dye their clothes as a way to deprive them of their colourful native dress.

The greatest example of the importance of saffron to European culture is, perhaps, *Crocologia*, the singular tome

dedicated entirely to saffron, written by Johann Ferdinand
Hertodt, a seventeenth-century German physician and writer.
An exhaustive exploration of saffron from its believed begin-
nings, the book recounts the spice's revered place in antiquity
through the Middle Ages, its use as a medicine, and as a flavouring for food and perfume. Hertodt's work was widely
referenced well into the nineteenth century by those studying
the saffron crocus.

A true saffron devotee, Hertodt, like many of his era,
believed in saffron's ability to cure all ills – from simple
toothache to depression, to, of course, plague. The book

An 18th-century
Italian botanical
guide's depiction
of saffron, in
Giorgio Bonelli,
*Hortus Romanus
secundum systema
J. P. Tournefortii*,
vol. VI (Rome,
1780).

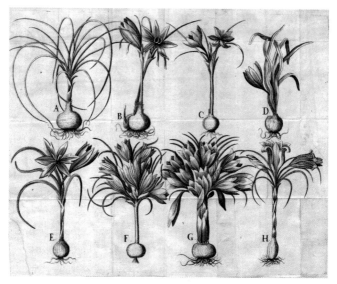

Hertodt's 17th-century tome is dedicated entirely to the history and uses of saffron. This illustration depicts its growth and proliferation cycles.

also gathered an extensive variety of saffron recipes, which, by the sixteenth and seventeenth centuries, were widely available, albeit by that time only for use in noble homes that could afford its luxury.

4
North America
and the Caribbean

What is consumed here comes chiefly from England.
Which by the proper cultivation they give it, is allowed
to be greatly superior to any other. It is a root that
will grow and thrive in any climate and almost any
soil; why then, when the cultivation is properly known,
may not a sufficient quantity be raised here for our own
consumption, if not for exportation. These roots or
bulbs are very cheap in England: how easily they might
be imported by the spring ships; when they would arrive
in proper time for cultivation.

John Spurrier, *The Practical Farmer* (1793)

The imperial leanings of European nations such as Britain, France, Holland, Spain and Portugal were initially based almost entirely on the social and commercial value of the spice trades to those nations. By the fifteenth century, when maritime advancements enabled ships to travel further and faster than ever before, European nations were desperately searching for a quicker route to India and the doorway it provided to the silk routes into China and the Middle East. Indeed, every school-child knows the story of Genoan Columbus's 1492 voyage under the flag of Spain, seeking a sea route to the East that would realize that nation's commercial hopes in cornering the spice trades.

Of course, every schoolchild also knows what happened: he didn't find a quicker route to the East Indies but reached the West Indies – the Caribbean – instead. There he found a variety of new spices and fruits – native chilli peppers, allspice, vanilla and pineapple. More compelling, he found an uncharted land that was hospitable to the transplant of the spices of the East – pepper berries, coffee, cinnamon and nutmeg. Suddenly, European cooks who were already using vast quantities of Eastern spices had new items to add to their repertoire and it was in their kitchens that the confluence of East and West began.

The promise of potential wealth in the West Indies of course set off a mad dash towards colonization, and soon Spain, Portugal, England and France were all laying claim to the islands of the Caribbean, Central and South America and the eastern shores of North America.

For those, such as the Spanish and Portuguese, whose native cuisines featured a healthy dose of saffron, it was a hardship to do without the spice when they settled as colonists in the New World. Soon enough, ships from the European motherlands carried this precious cargo – insured and commoditized ounce for ounce at the price of gold – to native sons and daughters who were developing vast wealth in the Caribbean with their plantations of coffee, sugar and cocoa, made successful on the backs of enslaved people from Africa. This saffron made its way north as well, as part of the triangular trade routes between the East and Africa, the Caribbean colonies to the North American colonies and back to Europe.

In Virginia, saffron was well used by affluent families like that of Martha Washington. Recipes using saffron appear in *Martha Washington's Booke of Cookery*, a family cookbook that was handwritten at some point during the seventeenth century before it was passed to her and then on to her granddaughter. Direction is given to use saffron steeped in rose water to colour marchpane (marzipan) fruits. Another recipe, for 'Spirit of Saffron' (saffron presumably distilled in liquor), indicates its uses for suppressing a 'trembling heart' and spleen obstructions. As in other accounts, it is indicated as good for melancholy and useful for travelling women – presumably to keep them calm in the uncomfortable travelling conditions of the period.

One recipe in the cookbook, for 'Aquimirabelis', or 'miracle water', said to cure a multitude of ills, was probably taken from John Gerard's *Herball; or, Generall Historie of Plantes*, a seventeenth-century tome that was popular for its advice on medicinal flowers and herbs. Aquimirabelis featured all manner of exotics, including cardamom, nutmeg and galangal, along with saffron:

To Make Aquimirabelis

Take 2 quarts [2 l] of sack; one pine of ye juice of sellandine; half a pine of ye Juice of mint; melilot flowers, rosasolis, cardimons, quibbibs, gallinggall mace nutmeggs, cloves, and ginger of each a dram; one handful of the flowers of Cowslips and a little saffron. Beat these alltogether, except ye cowslips and saffron, and mix them with ye sack and Juice overnight. and distill it leasurely in a cold still, pasteing the sides close, & let it drop upon some white sugar or sugar candy, which you put into your receiving bottle or swetten as you use it.[1]

Translated, the recipe calls for 470 ml (1 pint) of the juice of the celandine poppy, which is still used today in Asia as a general detoxifier; half a pint of mint juice, which we can assume is a tisane of mint and water; melilot flowers, a native North American legume now known to contain coumarin, a blood thinner; and rosasolis, a tincture made from the carnivorous sundew plant, which was said to have aphrodisiac properties. These are beaten together with a dram (about 1.7 g/ ⅛ oz) each of nutmeg, quibibs (a type of pepper), galangal, mace, nutmeg, cloves and ginger. These are then mixed with sack, a white fortified wine, along with cowslips, a perennial herb thought to have magical properties, before the saffron is added. The mixture is allowed to steep overnight then distilled in a cold slow still before being poured over sugar into its container.

Saffron would not be cultivated domestically in North America until the first half of the eighteenth century, when the Schwenkfelders immigrated to the New World. According to *The Schwenkfelders of Pennsylvania*, written by Selina Schultz, it was the Schultz family who brought the saffron crocus to Pennsylvania via Holland in 1730. The Schultzes were fleeing religious persecution in Saxony for espousing the teachings of Caspar Schwenkfeld, a late fifteenth–early sixteenth-century Protestant reformer who advocated a more moderate practice of Christianity than Martin Luther.

The Schultz family member who made it to North America would become the father of Pennsylvania saffron production. He was one of three brothers, another of whom remained in Holland, while the third set off to work in the East India trade. On arrival in the Pennsylvania colony, the Schwenkfelders made eastern Pennsylvania and the Susquehanna River Valley their home, where they became known as the 'Pennsylvania Dutch'.

Among their precious few worldly goods, the Schwenkfelders carried the saffron corms of which they were so fond to the New World, and by 1730 they were harvesting enough in their new homeland for use in their traditional dishes, earning themselves a variation on their new name: *Geelder Deutsch*, literally 'Golden' or 'Yellow German'.

The value of Geelder Deutsch saffron became readily apparent, and it was only a matter of time before these skilled merchants understood the wealth-creating potential of what they had. It was easy enough to send saffron to the port of Philadelphia, where ships engaged in trade with the Caribbean plied molasses, spices and enslaved people. By the end of the eighteenth century and the beginning of the nineteenth, saffron of the Schwenkfelders and their religious anabaptist cousins, the Mennonites, was regularly travelling to the West Indian colonies – a business that lasted all the way to 1812, when the naval war with England of that year ended commerce between its colonies and the new American republic. All commerce stopped as British blockades of the Caribbean, similar to those during the American Revolution, prevented trade with the newly founded United States.

Even though that lucrative avenue of sale was closed off, saffron remained an important part of the cultural life of these German immigrants and their descendants. They continued to sell saffron, both as a spice and as corms for others to propagate locally in their communities, as evidenced by nineteenth-century advertisements for its sale at local mercantiles and, later, drugstores and pharmacies like that in Lititz, Pennsylvania, which remains the saffron capital of America.

A local folk art blossomed around saffron as well, with the creation of hand-carved and, later, painted wooden boxes and jars for its storage. Today these are collectible antiques that can fetch hundreds of dollars each. Among the most sought-after are those made by Joseph Lehn in the nineteenth century.

SAFFRON.

Copyright 1879 by L. Prang & Co. Boston, U.S.A

Trade card for
R. & J. Gilchrist,
dry goods, 1879,
Boston.

Mildred Ford, *Pa. German Saffron Box*, c. 1941, watercolour, graphite and gouache on paper. Pennsylvania Dutch saffron growers created traditional boxes to house the precious crocus threads.

Martin Keen, the Lancaster, Pennsylvania, farmer and Mennonite who spent a decade growing saffron for commercial sale, notes that his ancestors even used saffron to treat animals on the farm, demonstrating how much store they placed on its curative properties. One such handwritten family recipe calls for warm milk straight from the cow mixed with saffron as a cure for farm dogs who may have ingested poisonous berries – although the exact proportions of any of the ingredients are not provided.

Even Thomas Jefferson got in on the saffron act – not as a commercial enterprise but as one of the many ornamentals he planted at Monticello, the Virginia estate where the third u.s. president indulged his love for amateur botany. The first shipment of saffron crocus to Monticello came in 1807 from Philadelphia horticulturist Bernard McMahon. One can guess with some certainty that McMahon is likely to have acquired the specimens from his Lancaster County neighbours.

5
Arts and Medicine

> Reduced to a powder it is used to perfume the theatre . . .
> there is also an eye salve that is indebted to this plant for its name
> . . . the lees of the extract of saffron, employed in the saffron
> unguent called 'crocomagma' have their own peculiar utility
> in cases of cataract.
>
> Pliny the Elder (23 CE–79 CE), *Natural History*

Measured against the price of gold since antiquity, saffron has almost always indisputably been the world's most expensive spice. But, unlike many other costly speciality ingredients, it has also been a triple and quadruple duty ingredient used in everything from food and medicine to clothing dyes, perfumes and cosmetics, as well as being the subject of literature and an ingredient in high art. In terms of value for money, saffron delivers.

In ancient Greece and Rome – and the outposts of those respective empires – saffron was considered effective for sweetening the air and was strewn lavishly in public spaces such as theatres and even thoroughfares ahead of important parades of dignitaries.

As the wall paintings at Thera suggest, the gathering and harvesting of saffron threads was an activity overseen by a

Fresco showing monkeys with croci, 1600–1450 BCE, Heraklion
Archaeological Museum, Crete.

goddess rather than mere mortals. Ancient Greek priestesses
and women of high status wore saffron-dyed robes. During
the Eleusinian Mysteries, a festival honouring the earth goddess Demeter and her daughter Persephone – who was
doomed to spend six months of the year in the underworld
as the kidnapped consort of her uncle Hades, god of the land
of the dead – there was a secret festival celebrating the minor
god Krokos.

Not much is known about the festival except that the
priests, who claimed Krokos as a direct ancestor, wore woven
woollen wristbands dyed with saffron. The story goes that at
some point, it seems that the youth Krokos (Crocus) had
morphed into a demi-deity after his metamorphosis into a
flower. This version of Krokos was perhaps related to another
variation of the myth in which the youth is particularly

Rakhsh, the legendary horse, in the 10th-century Persian epic by Abu' l-Qasim Firdowsi Tusi, *Shâhnâmeh* (The Book of Kings), 1616, was described as having a saffron-dappled coat.

beloved by the god Hermes, who accidentally kills him and turns him into the small, purple flower.

As it made its way through the silk trade routes deeper into the East, saffron captured the imaginations of its new devotees in religion as well. When saffron reached the Indian subcontinent, it proved a perfectly adaptable symbolic representation for fire and the purity it was believed to bring in Hindu religious ceremonies. The similarity to the ancient Persian Zoroastrian belief in fire as the most sanctified representation of the deity cannot be ignored, especially as it was the Persian Empire that first successfully cultivated and exported mass quantities of saffron to neighbouring lands.

Persian saffron also made its way into that culture's literature in the tenth-century Persian epic *Shâhnâmeh* (Book of Kings), in which the poet Ferdowsi records the legendary tales of Persian mythology in poetic form. He describes the main hero Rustam's trusty stallion Rakhsh – a horse, it was said, with the strength and bravery to kill a lion – as having a coat that was the colour of 'rose petals scattered upon a saffron ground'.[1] Later illustrated manuscripts likely used saffron dye to approximate Rakhsh's colour.

Soon after saffron's arrival in India, Hindu priests were using it not only to flavour offerings, but to dye their robes. This is similar to the robes worn by many Buddhist monks, Buddhism having originated in India and then been exported widely throughout eastern Asia between the sixth and fourth centuries BCE.

Theravada monks at Boudha in Kathmandu, Nepal, in their saffron-coloured robes.

This practice is remarked on in the fourteenth-century text *The Travels of Sir John Mandeville*, a self-proclaimed knight who claimed to have travelled throughout the Middle and Far East, India and some of Africa as part of his mission as a Crusader. In the manuscript – now largely considered entirely a work of fiction – under a chapter entitled 'Of Their Temples and Idols: and how they behave themselves in Worshipping their False gods', he describes a religion of the 'Jugures' who live near 'Organum' and into Persia.

The priests, he writes, wear saffron-coloured robes and have shaven heads and faces.[2] The description suggests a keen resemblance to the robes worn by Buddhist monks and Hindu priests, but the (likely imagined) city names make the narrative hard to place. Nonetheless, what we can glean from this fanciful tale is how powerful the image of the saffron-robed priest of the East was, even in the Middle Ages, given that it bore mention in the would-be Crusader's tale.

At various Indian religious festivals, whether Hindu, Jain, Muslim or Christian, desserts coloured and flavoured with

Peda, a South Asian sweet that uses saffron and is commonly eaten at holy festivals.

saffron are offered to celebrants. In these special holy events, it is the saffron of Kashmir that is considered most desirable. One third-century Chinese medical text refers to saffron as being grown in Kashmir to be acquired and used 'for the primary purpose of offering to the Buddha'.[3] In Hinduism and Jainism, libations of saffron, milk and other spices are offered to statues of deities.

One of the more dramatic examples is at the Jain Gomateshwara festival, which takes place every twelve years in Shravanabelagola in the Indian state of Karnataka. There, a 17-m-tall (57 ft) statue of Bahubali, the son of the first and most revered teacher of Jainism, is anointed with saffron milk poured by the devout from a large scaffold constructed around the statue. Espousing a predominantly vegetarian lifestyle, Jainism is based on a spiritual path that practises non-violence, asceticism, celibacy, truth and, among other things, non-extravagance.

In the twentieth century, when India had gained its independence from the British Empire and adopted its own flag, the use of orange representing the hue of saffron as one of its official colours was a clear choice, given the spice's importance in a variety of Indian religions.

From its earliest cultivation, religion provided an excellent segue for saffron to make the transition to art. In the seventh century, the wall paintings at Thera in Greece not only depict saffron gathering as a religiously sanctioned experience, but make use of saffron as a pigment, as it was more than fifty millennia ago in wall paintings in what is today Iraq.

Even though saffron use had waned in Europe after the fall of the Roman Empire in 476 CE until the Crusades in the twelfth century, it still made an appearance in the labour-intensive religious texts of the Catholic Church, such as the Book of Kells, an illuminated manuscript painstakingly

The Jain Gomateshwara festival is held once every dozen years at Shravanabelagola in the Indian state of Karnataka. Held since the year 981 BCE, worshippers pour saffron water or saffron milk onto a 17-m (57 ft) statue of Gomateshwara, a revered figure in the Jain religion, from a specially constructed platform.

Saffron was adopted as an official colour of the Indian flag with the formation of the Indian republic in 1947, due to its significance in the Hindu, Jain and Buddhist religions.

produced by the monastery of St Columba, an Irish abbot who lived in the sixth century CE. The manuscript, which comprises the four Gospels of the New Testament, along with other material, was written in either Britain or Ireland in the ninth century CE. Recent analysis shows that saffron was responsible for the golden colouring used throughout the book.

Similarly, Indian and Persian miniatures, as well as those of the Mogul Empire, which originated in modern-day Uzbekistan and spread to Afghanistan, northern India and Iran in the sixteenth century, used saffron for their orange hue but, perhaps more interestingly, also as a stabilizer for the verdigris used for green tints in these paintings and manuscript pages. It is saffron that has allowed these colours to remain vibrant today – in some cases as much as five hundred years after they were produced. Modern scientists have determined that the

Saffron was used as a dye in medieval illuminated manuscripts such as the *Book of Kells* (521–97 CE), Folio 32v, MS 58.

reason lies in the chemicals safranal, the organic compound from which saffron gets its smell, and crocetin, a natural acid present in the stigmas of the saffron crocus.[4]

In one early eighteenth-century miniature from Rajasthan, used to illustrate a ragmala – a poem of twelve verses

Rostam sleeping while Rakhsh, his saffron-dappled horse, fights a lion, from Abu 'l-Qasim Firdowsi Tusi, *Shâhnâmeh* (The Book of Kings), 1515–22, miniature.

Modern analysis indicates that Mogul-era miniatures like this one of *c.* 1590 resisted corrosion and fading in part because of the mixing of saffron with various pigments.

– we get to see saffron do triple duty, not only as a colorant, but as a fixative to the greenish hues and as part of the poetic ode of the depicted scene:

> Her sari, soaked with kesara [saffron], is enchanting. [Her] musk caste mark at the forehead bewitches the mind. The lovable [woman has] matted locks and ash in her[?] palms. [She has] smeared srikhands [white sandalwood paste] all over her body. The trident in her arm is resplendent. Such is the beauty of Bangali.[5]

Even William Shakespeare saw fit to pay homage to saffron. Its importance to English Renaissance society is made clear by his words in *The Winter's Tale*, Act IV, Scene 3, when the clown states that he 'must have saffron to colour the warden pies'. Warden pies were an open-faced tart made from a hard pear and saffron grown by monks near the town of Old Warden in Bedfordshire.

In 1624 the Swiss writer and etcher Matthäus Merian the Elder composed an entire poem in German to the saffron crocus to accompany his engraving of a beautiful garden with a large saffron crocus in the foreground. Merian was from Basel, the Swiss city that had some success in the medieval period growing and trading its own saffron.

Science may be the counterpoint to art but, as we have seen, saffron has always been well represented in that realm as well – sometimes almost beyond the bounds of believability. It has been considered as everything from an aphrodisiac to a solution for acne, yet modern scientists have proven at least some of the medical folklore surrounding saffron to be right.

For example, ancient texts consistently say of saffron that it causes a 'quickening' of the heart or the blood. In 2014 a team at Mashhad University in Iran undertook the compiling

Bangali Ragini: folio from a ragamala series (*Garland of Musical Modes*), 1709. The Amber ragamala text of which this work is a part offers the following description of this ragini: 'Her sari, soaked with kesara [saffron], is enchanting.'

A field surrounded by wooded hills, with a saffron crocus in the foreground and a poem beneath. Etching by Matthäus Merian der Ältere, c. 1629.

of the various ancient ills said to be cured by saffron.[6] The list is almost comically long:

> In traditional medicine in various countries, saffron has been used for various purposes including analgesic and anti-inflammatory (earache, tooth-ache, swelling, otitis, anal pain, gout, cancer pain, gingivitis, discomfort of teething infants), cardiovascular system (cardiac stimulant, removes blockages of vascular), central nervous system (narcotic, antihysteric, CNS stimulant, hypnotic, mental disease, sedative, anticonvulsant, neurasthenia), eye disease (painful eye, lacrimation, day blindness,

corneal disease and cataract, purulent eye infection,
pterygium, poor vision), gastrointestinal system (sto-
machic, anorexia, treatment of hemorrhoid, prolapse
of anus, jaundice, and enlargement of the liver, anti-
flatulent), genitourinary system (abortion, treatment of
amenorrhea, aphrodisiac, impotency, emmenagogue,
stimulate menstruation, prolapse of anus, stop menstrual

periods, promote menstruation, use in puerperium period, terminate pregnancy, painful urination, diuretic, kidney stone), infection disease (antibacterial, antiseptic, anti-fungal, measles, smallpox, scarlet fever), respiratory system (asthma, bronchitis, expectorant, pertussis, dyspnea, pleurisy, antitussive, diphtheria, disability tonsils resulting snoring, respiratory decongestant, expectorant), skin disease (treatment of psoriasis, eczema, acne, wound), and miscellaneous (immunostimulant, diaphoretic, tissue coloration, anticancer).[7]

More interesting, perhaps, is the equally long list of modern research trials in which saffron is currently taking centre stage:

> Various pharmacological activities of saffron and its constituents have been extensively studied including anti-cancer, antidepressant, anti-Parkinson, anti-Alzheimer, anticonvulsant, anti-ischemic (such as brain, kidney, muscular and heart ischemia), anti-hypertensive, anti-genotoxic, and antidote (e.g. against snake venom, diazinon, acrylamide or acrolein), antitussive, hypolipidemic, antioxidant, antinociceptive, and anti-inflammatory effects. Some clinical studies about saffron and its constituents have been cited in the literature such as safety evaluation, aphrodisiac, antidepressant, and anti-Alzheimer effects.[8]

In 2016, researchers from four Japanese universities found that crocin had neuroprotective qualities.[9] In 2018, scientists at the Department of Vascular Surgery at the Attikon Hospital, part of the National and Kapodistrian University of Athens, determined through a series of clinical studies that saffron has anti-inflammatory properties useful for stabilizing arterial plaque, a leading cause of high blood pressure and heart disease.[10]

Unlike many legendary cures, the lore of saffron's therapeutic powers seems to have, at least in some cases, a strong foundation in truth, and it is safe to say that many more studies exploring its pharmaceutical potential will continue to be undertaken. As in the past, it remains to be seen how medical breakthroughs – or beliefs – will affect the price of the world's already costliest spice.

6

The Modern Market

It takes about 150,000 flowers to produce a kilogram
(2.2 pounds) of saffron. Little wonder, then, that the precious
powder has spawned a trade rife with the kind of deceptions
and distortions typical of traffic in gems or illicit drugs: cheap
substitutes, diluted shipments, false labeling. Today, a battle
over the future of the 'gold of cuisine' is underway, as its world
is transformed by speculation and market upheaval.

Elaine Sciolino, 'A New Chapter For Saffron', *New York Times*,

28 December 2015

What is considered a luxury good changes dramatically with
time and availability. Once, both common black pepper and
salt were so costly that wages and debts were paid in their
measure. When potatoes travelled from South America to
Europe, the crop was so coveted that the king of France had
his potato patch under armed guard. Saffron, on the other
hand, is probably one of the few commodities that has never
lost the huge value or almost mythical allure it was assigned
in antiquity. Even when the cost of gold fluctuates, saffron's
high price tag remains steady.

The main reason, of course, is that saffron is incredibly
laborious to harvest. It remains one of the few crops that has

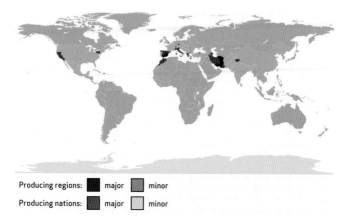

Producing regions: ▮ major ▮ minor
Producing nations: ▮ major ▮ minor

The world's primary saffron-producing nations and regions.

not benefitted from automation – perhaps because of the delicacy of the operation of plucking the thread-like stigmas from the flower. It is hard to imagine how this task that requires the most delicate touch, paired with sharp precision, could ever be taken over by machines, but only time will tell. Estimates hypothesize that about four hundred hours of human labour are needed to produce just 1 kg (2 lb 3 oz) of saffron.[1]

Saffron pickers work against the clock, since the saffron-picking window is a small one: the flower only blooms in the autumn, and the best time to harvest – right after the morning dew has evaporated – limits opportunity further.

Another issue with saffron growing is its areas of cultivation. Historically, few climates have presented the perfect conditions to grow saffron, although stalwart devotees have tried to grow it in virtually every corner of the world – with more success in some areas than others. In modern times, climate change is potentially redrawing the map of saffron-growing zones, often to the detriment of regions historically known for growing saffron and where saffron culture is an integral part of local heritage.

Pampore in the Indian region of Kashmir is often considered to be the producer of the world's best-quality saffron. The Food and Agriculture Organization of the United Nations has named this region of saffron cultivation, and regions in Iran and Afghanistan, to be Globally Important Agricultural Heritage Systems. The GIAHS designation serves in much the same way as AOC in France (Appellation d'origine contrôlée, or label of controlled origin) or DOC (Denominazione di origine protetta, or label of protected origin) in Italy do – to verify the authenticity and purity of the food product in question. Another aspect of the designation is that it recognizes how integral the farming systems or crops in the GIAHS area are to the fabric of local society in a cultural sense as well.

However, excessive drought and political conflict is having an impact on the Kashmiri harvest. In the 1990s, a single

Harvesting saffron continues to be a labour-intensive task done by hand.

Kashmiri farmer could produce up to 400 kg (around 880 lb) of saffron per year. Production dropped to half that amount a decade ago. In 2018 farmers were reporting crop yields that amounted to less than 10 kg (22 lb) for the entire year. Add to that the fact that Kashmir is the world's most militarized zone – a Muslim territory in India that, though granted autonomy over seventy years ago, is under continual occupation, with a conflict death toll numbering in the tens of thousands – and saffron growers find it increasingly hard to engage in their trade. Saffron is high on the list of what modern culinary scholars call 'conflict food': traditional food customs that are being irrevocably altered by social, political or military conflict in a given region.

In 2019 the Indian government rescinded Kashmir's regional autonomy and added even more troops to the area, severing the state's communication with the outside world. Between climate crisis and political crisis, saffron cultivation in this region is bracing for potential extinction, and aficionados can expect to pay ever-escalating prices for what little Kashmiri saffron threads make it out of the region, usually in the hands of smugglers.

On the flip side, it was military conflict that renewed saffron farming in Afghanistan, a nation that has been a conflict zone since the 1970s, when Soviet and later Islamic fundamentalist influences brought war and foreign military engagement to the country. Afghanistan later became a battleground in the prolonged Western fight against fundamentalist-based terrorism. During that time, it was opium that provided a living to Afghan farmers but, today, government efforts are turning opium fields into fields of purple crocus flowers. The plants are being grown in the Kandahar region in the province of Herat, where mild winters and dry summers are suitable for it to thrive.

Saffron growing is considered a heritage agricultural activity in Kashmir.

One major exporter of saffron, Rumi Spice, was started by three U.S. Army veterans who had been stationed in Afghanistan during their military service. After appearing on the American television show *Shark Tank*, in which entrepreneurs pitch business ideas to successful business people in the hope of being awarded venture capital, the trio received U.S.$250,000 of seed money to start their saffron concern. Today the company works directly with Afghan farmers to bring not only saffron but saffron-related products to the United States, where total saffron sales account for about U.S.$60 million of all total spice sales as compared to a worldwide market valued at about US$10 billion.

Often, in saffron-growing regions, women and children are recruited to harvest saffron because they can be paid the least, owing to cultural perceptions of their lesser status. Indian celebrity chef-turned-film director Vikas Khanna is currently working on a film that portrays the difficult lives of child saffron labourers in the valleys of north India. Rumi

Spice, on the other hand, employs nearly 2,000 women at a living wage in Herat to harvest and package saffron. For many women in this Islamic country, it is the first and probably only opportunity to find work outside their homes.

The company founders say that, in addition to a lucrative business, their work is a mission of peace, offering economic security to a land desperate for stability. This literal and figurative hunger has, in the past, led poor Afghan farmers to be willing accomplices in the opium drug trade rather than let their families starve. By growing saffron, these farmers are now able to feed another, far less nefarious addiction – that of the gourmand. Rumi Spice also claim to invest a large percentage of their proceeds back into manufacturing and agricultural infrastructure in the Afghan growing regions they work with, thereby creating continued and increasing employment opportunity for locals.

The success of companies like Rumi Spice speak to the growing American interest in procuring saffron, which had

Saffron cultivation is a major industry in Iran.

In Iran, saffron growing is a corporate versus cottage industry.

become more costly and difficult over the course of nearly forty years. This was largely due to the fact that there was no direct import of saffron from Iran – the world's largest saffron grower – because of sanctions put into place by the United States following the 1979 Islamic Revolution in that country. Iran produces 90 per cent of the world's saffron.

During the time of the embargo, saffron smuggling into the United States became a lucrative business, but those few sellers who had the wherewithal to bring Iranian saffron in through legal ports of entry such as Canada benefitted as well. Countries like Spain, which produces very little saffron but retains a strong association with the spice, would buy Iranian saffron and repackage it as their own. At one point, when saffron production by Pennsylvania Dutch farmers in America was at its peak in the eighteenth and early nineteenth centuries, even that saffron was labelled 'Spanish Saffron', for sale in the Caribbean and local sale as well. While sanctions against Iranian saffron were lifted by the United States in 2016, leading American saffron-lovers to rejoice, rebranding of Iranian saffron still continues.

The availability of Iranian saffron hasn't necessarily affected efforts to smuggle the spice, particularly to areas where saffron is an integral part of the cultural fabric. In India, for example, where saffron is used in Hindu religious rites, the decline of Kashmiri saffron production has been a hardship. While Iranian saffron is plentiful, high importation duties make it costly. Black-market saffron is brought into the country by human 'mules', who, like drug mules, are smuggling the contraband into the nation in hidden suitcase compartments.

In any given year, Indian newspapers report the seizure of drugs, gold and saffron at national airports. It is, however, a black-market business that goes both ways – Indian growers attempting to produce a better-quality product than even Kashmiri saffron work as diligently to get the threads out of the country to a lucrative international market as those who seek to get cheaper saffron *in* to the country for local use.

To increase its appeal, saffron smuggled into and out of India is often relabelled – usually as Kashmiri – in order to fetch the highest price. However, the relabelling of saffron – Iranian as Spanish, for example – is also common and perfectly legal.

This relabelling of saffron from acknowledged growing regions is an issue that is at the least misrepresentation and at the most fraud. Throughout history, the unscrupulous have looked for ways to doubly capitalize on saffron's value by adulterating it or offering cheap substitutes masquerading as the real thing. In 2019 British authorities in Sussex seized £750,000 of the fake stuff – real saffron stigmas mixed with other matter to bulk it up. In that particular case, the adulteration was traced to a saffron factory in Spain rather than on-the-ground tampering after import.

The organic matter most often passed off as saffron – either in a mix with the real spice or on its own – is marigold and safflower petals, which are often marketed as Egyptian or Mexican saffron but which can include any number of organic and inorganic fillers.

The most common substitute or 'false' saffron has been turmeric. A rhizome in the ginger family, turmeric resembles ginger and galangal roots but has vibrant orange flesh. This can be used fresh, usually grated, or dried into a powder. It is turmeric that gives Indian and Thai yellow curries their hue. Turmeric, like saffron, has a certain astringency, but the flavour and aroma are very different and for dishes that require the specific taste of saffron, it is not a comparable substitute.

The thirteenth-century Venetian merchant-explorer Marco Polo observed the use of turmeric as a substitute for saffron in China, writing in his travel log,

> There is also vegetable that has all the properties of the true saffron, as well as the color, and yet is not really saffron. It is held in great estimation and being an ingredient in all their dishes, it bears, on that account, a high price.[2]

The belief in the capacity of turmeric to substitute for saffron is still pervasive today. Interestingly, in the Caribbean nation of Trinidad and Tobago, turmeric is marketed and labelled as 'saffron', even though turmeric itself is valued for its own properties. Turmeric called 'saffron' is key to the nation's cuisine, which is heavily influenced by the East Indian-descent population of that nation, most of whose ancestors were indentured labourers originating from northern India, where true saffron was at least presumably known to them.

Some two hundred years after Marco Polo travelled to China, Europeans were taking measures to prevent the counterfeiting of saffron. We know that Henry viii of England banned the use of saffron as a very expensive hair dye, but it was Henry ii of France who set forth a series of laws to prevent the sale of false saffron:

> For some time past a certain quantity of the said saffron has been found altered, disguised, and sophisticated, by being mixed with oil, honey, and other mixtures, in order that the said saffron, which is sold by weight, may be rendered heavier; and some add to it other herbs, similar in colour and substance to beef over-boiled, and reduced to threads which saffron, thus mixed and adulterated, cannot be long kept, and is highly prejudicial to the human body; which, besides the said injury may prevent the above-said foreign merchants from purchasing

Saffron is used extensively in Persian cooking and there are some shops in Iran entirely dedicated to selling the spice.

Turmeric is often used as a colour substitute for saffron.

it, to the great diminution of our revenues, and to the great detriment of foreign nations, against which we ought to provide.[3]

The drive to procure a reliable source of saffron that is both pure and unaffected by foreign politics or markets remains as strong today as it did throughout antiquity, the Middle Ages and the Renaissance.

In North America, encouraged by the historical success of the Pennsylvania Dutch, these efforts have ramped up in recent years and in unexpected locations. Notably, the University of Vermont's North American Center for Saffron Research and Development provides a continuously growing resource for would-be American saffron farmers, including everything from educational seminars about the history and trade of saffron to growing and cultivation advice, to recipes and product development. The centre even runs an online forum for saffron farmers, Saffronnet.

The centre encourages the perfection of hoop- or 'high tunnel'-based farming and planting under solar panels as a way to grow saffron successfully in cold-weather climates. Farmers in Maine are experimenting with growing saffron using these methods, drawn by the fact that it is an autumn to early winter crop that could provide revenue after the summer growing and harvesting season has finished.

Even as far north as Canada, farmers are trying their luck with saffron. In 2014 Pur Safran was the first saffron farm to open in Canada, and today the farm not only sells its own saffron; it sells saffron soap and corms, and in 2019 it opened an academy to teach others how to grow and harvest the plant.

Northern California's Peace & Plenty saffron farm opened in 2017 and grew 325 g (11½ oz) of saffron to sell in 2019, with plans to increase production to a kilogram (2.2 lb) by 2020. They also sell saffron corms, but, perhaps more interestingly, the proprietors offer farm stays, tapping into the age-old allure and romance of being among purple fields of saffron croci.

On the other side of the world, New Zealand has a growing number of large-scale domestic producers, and smaller farmers in Essex, England, are working hard to bring back what was once a booming medieval industry centred around towns like Saffron Walden. In the Netherlands, a country known for its skill in growing the world's most abundant and beautiful varieties of tulips, growers are leveraging their knowledge of growing this bulb-based plant to try to grow saffron from corms. The first harvest and export of Dutch saffron happened in 2019. Persistent individuals have even tried – albeit with limited luck – growing saffron at high elevations in subtropical climates, which are normally inhospitable to the saffron crocus.

What has brought about the new millennium interest in growing saffron outside its traditional growing areas? Certainly, the interest in saffron cultivation could be called a modern-day gold rush towards a crop with a higher price per pound than any other, but other forces are surely at play for saffron to be pursued so earnestly in regions with no social or cultural association with the plant and its role in cuisine, religion, art or medicine.

For gourmands devoted to an eat-local lifestyle, locally grown saffron is an attractive way to have an incomparable spice normally grown far from home. However, for the most part, it's the pursuit of health that is making saffron so attractive – as it has off and on for millennia. Certainly, there are scientists researching saffron's potential in a variety of illnesses, but aficionados of popular, trendy medical advice are also hailing saffron power for everything from weight loss to curing Alzheimer's and Attention Deficit Hyperactivity Disorder (ADHD). According to a study by Market Research Reports.biz, a research firm based in Albany, New York, the market for capsules or tablets of concentrated saffron as a food supplement targeted towards health consumers is expected to see huge growth well into 2025.[4] Saffron day creams, night creams, and body and massage oils are in high demand in South and East Asia and are an increasingly growing market. Small, artisanal producers in the West are beginning to explore this market segment as well.

Indeed, much of the advertising language used to market these new saffron supplements and beauty products includes words like 'miraculous' and 'magical' – just as they did thousands of years ago when saffron sellers were marketing the spice as Alexander the Great's secret health weapon.

Whether or not saffron can cure a variety of human ills remains to be seen – this is a question that must be answered by scientists. But regardless of its promise as a panacea, one thing is true of saffron: it remains firmly entrenched in the imagination and hearts of those who experience it as the queen of spices.

Risotto is made in the Milanese style when it features saffron.

A Saffron Primer

It is an herb of the Sun, and under the Lion. Saffron is endowed
with great virtues, for it refreshes the spirits, and is good against
fainting-fits and the palpitation of the heart.

Culpeper's Complete Herbal (1653)

For those who have become charmed by the world's most
expensive spice, no substitute will do. Indeed, those classic
dishes that feature saffron almost seem to be built around its
fine threads of red gold, rather than the other way around.
Saffron is no mere flavouring or addition to a dish, it is the
dish's raison d'être. In an almost-magical way, the heady yet
clean aroma and the vibrant hue of saffron bring an essence
to food that is incomparable.

Despite the fact that there are no substitutes for saffron,
there are many pretenders to the throne, and the temptation to
use one of them to replace this costly ingredient can be strong.

Indian-American food writer Monica Bhide, who is known
for her expertise on spices, writes that the most common
question she receives from her readers is about saffron – but
not about how to use it. Instead, said Bhide, when I inter-
viewed her in 2019, readers consistently ask how to substitute
saffron or whether they can simply do without it because of

its cost and because of a general lack of understanding about how exactly to use it.

Bhide counts herself among those saffron aficionados who advise strongly against substituting saffron with another spice: rather than substitute saffron, simply leave it out. Or, as some of the most diehard will advise you, just don't make the dish at all.

But if you are going to drop a pretty penny on procuring your saffron, then buyer beware of counterfeits. This primer will help you avoid buying false goods.

Buying Saffron: A How To

Saffron is graded on three major qualities: its aroma (safranal), its strength as a colourant (crocin) and its taste (picrocrocin). Saffron is further graded by the quality of the stigma, with all-red stigmas being Grade 1 or A+; Grade 2 or A contain the red stigmas and a bit of the yellow or white base (style); Grade 3 or B is bunched saffron with the entire style attached. These grades are named differently for Spanish and Iranian varieties as follows:

Iranian

Iran produces 90 per cent of the world's saffron, and Iranian (Persian) saffron is generally considered to be the best quality behind the rarer Kashmiri saffron. It is graded as follows:

Super Negin: Most robust in aroma and flavour, this saffron contains only red threads that are uniformly trimmed. As such, there is less breakage or powdering of the saffron in the package. This is the most expensive and desirable grade of Iranian saffron.

Sargol: Literally translated from the Persian language of Farsi as 'the flower's head', this saffron comes from the red tips of the stigma without any yellow or white threads (styles). As a result, this saffron is quite short and the colour a deep red. The aroma is quite strong. Sargol saffron can break or crumble in the package because its lack of length makes it less supple, but it is still considered a high-quality saffron.

Negin: This saffron contains yellow and orange portions of the stigmas and is generally longer than the Super Negin and Sargol grades. The quality is still good but the presence of the yellow and orange stigma portions will affect the intensity of colour, aroma and taste.

Poshal: This saffron is the least expensive and comprises the orange and yellow parts of the crocus stigmas, generally considered the saffron 'trim'. While still technically saffron, this is the cheapest quality of saffron and is considered an inferior product.

Spanish

The Spanish region of La Mancha accounts for only 4 per cent of the saffron grown in the world, yet it exports 40 per cent of the world's saffron. How does this maths add up? Because Spain acts as middleman for Iranian saffron, which was largely impeded from distribution because of worldwide sanctions after that country's Islamic Revolution in 1979. As a result, the grades of Iranian saffron are rebranded in Spain as follows: Sargol = Coupe; Poshal = La Mancha. Actual La Mancha saffron grown in Spain will carry a Denomination of Protected Origin (DOP), which serves to ensure the authenticity of this rare and protected version of the spice. Regardless of country of origin of the product, saffron vendors are

Saffron, tumeric and curry displayed in a market in Granada, Spain.

required to hold certificates of origin for saffron, so buyers who want to know exactly where their saffron comes from can ask for this documentation.

Kashmiri

Grown in the Pampore region of Kashmir, a Muslim state in India, Kashmiri saffron is widely considered to be the finest quality in the world. Unlike Persian or Spanish saffron, which is most often presented as single stigmas, Kashmiri saffron is usually sold in a loose tangle. There are two varieties: one in which the yellowish-white 'style' (a tube-like stalk) is still attached to the stigma, considered the lesser of the two varieties; the second variety is pure stigma. Kashmiri saffron threads are extremely long, with a thick head and an exceptionally deep red colour. The sizes of these stigmas indicate the inherent suitability of the soil and climate in Kashmir for growing this product. The difference between this and other saffron is so marked that saffron from this region can usually be discerned by observation alone. Already the costliest saffron on the modern market, drought and political strife have limited production over the last decade, which will, no doubt, continue to drive prices up further.

Testing the Quality of Saffron

Saffron-lovers will gladly pay the steep price for a few ounces of the good stuff, and unscrupulous counterfeiters are always looking for ways to capitalize on this passion with cheap substitutes. Some of the products masquerading as saffron include safflower; sliced, dyed calendula flowers; dyed hay; corn silk and even thinly sliced onion skins that have been dyed or enhanced with paprika and turmeric. Labels for false saffron can vary, and include Egyptian, Mexican or American saffron. It should be noted, however, that there exists perfectly legitimate American saffron from Lancaster County, Pennsylvania, and new experimental growing regions. Yet, even without certificates of origin, there are ways to test the quality of saffron to ensure it is the real thing.

Water test: While hot water will help along the steeping of saffron, pure saffron will easily give up its colour to cold water. True saffron will release its colour slowly – it can take as long as fifteen minutes to steep fully. The colour imparted by real saffron is a deep yellow to orange colour rather than red, and even after steeping, the threads should not fully lose their colour. If your saffron threads turn clear or white after steeping, it's not the real thing.

Rub it: Take a couple of threads between two fingers and rub them back and forth. Real saffron threads will not break easily.

Taste it: Real saffron will smell sweet but never taste sweet. Place a thread in your mouth – if it tastes sweet, it's not the real thing.

Smell it: Pure saffron has an astringent, clean smell with slightly sweet undertones.

A Word about Powdered Saffron

Powdered saffron is often the most readily available type of saffron in standard supermarkets. It usually comes in a small, dark-coloured, air-sealed envelope that is then placed inside a spice jar. Because of its high price, some supermarkets will keep saffron behind a counter rather than in the spice aisle, but this is increasingly rare. Buyers should note, however, that powdered saffron is easier to adulterate than saffron threads. This might include mixing with other deep-red spices such as paprika, or simply dying organic matter as filler with the saffron. If possible, it's best to buy your saffron as whole threads and grind them yourself.

Where to Buy It

The following producers offer pure, unadulterated saffron. You may buy directly from these importers online or visit their websites for retailers local to you. Saffron is sold on websites such as amazon.co.uk, but before you buy, do a little

True saffron will release its colour immediately and intensely, particularly in warm water.

digging to ensure it comes from a reputable seller such as those below:

Zaran Saffron: Importers of Spanish and Persian saffron, zaransaffron.com

Rumi Spice: Afghan saffron, rumispice.com

Penzeys Spices: Sells Spanish Coupe grade saffron, penzeys. com

Kalustyan's, 123 Lexington Avenue, NY, foodsofnations.com. Kalustyan's has been providing Middle Eastern and South Asian spices and goods to New Yorkers since 1944, including a wide variety of saffron from the most noted producing regions.

GoldenSaffron.com

Saffron spices can be found in the UK at:

SaffronSpicesUK: www.saffronspices.co.uk

The Cheshire Saffron Company: British-grown saffron, www.cheshiresaffron.co.uk

Norfolk Saffron: grown at the north Norfolk coast, www.norfolksaffron.co.uk

Peace & Plenty Farm, California saffron growers, peace-plentyfarm.com

A Saffron-growing Manual

Martin Keen, the descendant of eighteenth-century Mennonite farmers in Lancaster, Pennsylvania, spent over a decade cultivating and selling the saffron grown on his farm as a way to diversify crops. Based on his advice, I have compiled this handy DIY guide for those hoping to grow saffron for their own use:

Know what you're buying: make sure you are purchasing *Crocus sativus*, which is also called the 'saffron crocus' or 'autumn crocus'. The common spring crocus (*Crocus vernus*) does not yield saffron stigmas.

Choosing your spot: Saffron croci like well-drained soil that is only moderately rich in organic matter. Saffron does not like wet, heavily rich soil.

Plant on time: Plant your saffron crocus corms from June to August, depending on your hardiness zone. Saffron can be planted from zones 6 to 9 in the United States and generally in areas where summer temperatures do not exceed 35°C or 40°C (95°F or 104°F) or dip below −15°C or −20°C (5°F or -4°F) in the winter.

Calculating how many to plant: It takes fifty to sixty saffron flowers to produce one tablespoon of saffron. Plan accordingly for how much saffron you'd like to harvest – and how much you can easily harvest without giving up. It's not easy work!

How to plant: Plant each corm 10 cm (4 in.) deep and 10 cm apart.

When to harvest: Once the purple flowers emerge and fully open, revealing the dark-red stigmas, the saffron flowers should be plucked early in the morning as soon as any dew has dried. Only harvest as many flowers as you can reasonably pluck stigmas from in one sitting. The flowers begin to fade and go bad very quickly.

How to harvest: Quickly pluck the stigmas from the flowers and set them on a tray lined with parchment paper. These are the saffron threads.

How to dry: Make sure the saffron threads are not piled on top of one another but are well spread out. Cover the tray with a thin sheet of white muslin and place in a warm, dry spot. After about three days, the saffron should be dry and brittle to the touch.

Dig up or separate?: Some people dig up the saffron corms at the end of their flowering period, but Martin Keen says they are fine to leave in the ground. By year five or six, they will be tightly packed, and that can make it hard to harvest. At that point, you may choose to dig up the corms, separate them gently and replant them.

Where to buy saffron corms: White Flower Farm (whiteflowerfarm.com); Dutch Grown (dutchgrown.com); Baker Creek Heirloom Seeds (rareseeds.com); RocoSaffron (the Netherlands) (rocosaffron.com); Sativus (the Netherlands) (sativus.com); RHS Plants (UK) (www.rhsplants.co.uk); Crocus UK (www.crocus.co.uk); English Saffron (UK) (englishsaffron.co.uk)

For small or home farmers looking to grow saffron, the North American Center for Saffron Research & Development at the University of Vermont offers a wealth of information, seminars and presentations, as well as a forum for saffron-growers called Saffronnet. Visit them at uvm.edu/~saffron.

Recipes

These recipes call for either saffron threads or ground saffron, depending on the preparation, but it should be stated that ground saffron will always produce a more intense colour and flavour. As such, you will want to adapt accordingly if you decide to substitute one for the other.

With respect to recipes, it is my opinion that it is best to purchase saffron threads versus saffron powder, which tends to lose its intensity more quickly. Store these in an airtight container, away from direct sunlight or intense heat.

Further, I have found that, unless you live in a particularly dry climate, you should consider lightly toasting your saffron threads before grinding, or you'll have a difficult time. Nothing is worse than soggy saffron threads that, ultimately, don't release the best colour or aroma. To toast your saffron, place the threads in a dry frying pan over a medium-low heat. Swirl them around in the pan for thirty to forty seconds. The threads may darken slightly, but don't allow them to darken too much. Remove from the heat and grind immediately. Adding a few grains of sugar to the mortar before grinding can help the process.

For those who would like to experiment with using saffron in less traditional recipes, I recommend taking a classic pairing approach. While some ingredients may certainly stray successfully out of their traditional 'comfort zone', saffron is a bit tricky because of its astringency and the delicacy of its flavour and aroma. Even in its strongest form, saffron risks being overwhelmed by heavier flavours, or even heavy-handed use of flavours with which it pairs well.

Traditionally, the flavours of the East, even when not used in Eastern or Middle Eastern preparations, work best with saffron: cumin, almonds, rice, tomato, lemon, potatoes, pistachio, fennel, fish, shellfish and chicken are some examples. As for pairing wine with saffron: drier whites usually work best.

Amish Saffron Chicken Soup and Rivels (Dumplings)

Mrs Charlene Van Brookhoven lives in Lititz, Pennsylvania, dubbed 'the coolest small town in America', a village in rural Lancaster County with a strong Pennsylvania Dutch heritage. Mrs Van Brookhoven's own Moravian German family immigrated to the area just after the Revolutionary War. While neither Amish nor Mennonite, this avid gardener, history lover and cook says she learned a few things from 'the simple folk', as they are sometimes locally called. Chief among these was how to grow the saffron crocus for her own culinary use in regionally popular recipes, such as this chicken soup with egg dumplings.

For the soup:
1 4-lb (1.8 kg) chicken cut into pieces
3 quarts (2.75 l) water
¼ tsp ground saffron
6 fresh cobs or 2 15-oz (400 g) cans of white corn, drained
1 tbsp freshly chopped parsley
3 hard-boiled eggs, diced
salt and freshly ground pepper to taste
canned or boxed chicken stock, as needed, if desired

For the rivels:
1 cup (125 g) all-purpose flour
pinch salt
1 egg, beaten

Place the chicken in a large stockpot and cover with the water, and add the salt. Bring to a boil and simmer until the meat is very tender, approximately 1½ hours. The meat should easily come away from the bones with a fork. Remove the chicken from the pot with a slotted spoon and allow to cool slightly until at an appropriate temperature to handle comfortably. Remove all the meat from the bones and set aside. Strain the stock through a fine mesh sieve into another pot; add the saffron and bring to the boil.

Make the rivels. Whisk the flour and salt together and add the egg. Mix until moistened. If too sticky, add more flour in very small amounts – about 1 teaspoon at a time – to achieve a very soft, pliable dough. Rub rivel dough between your hands to form quarter-sized pieces into the boiling stock, stirring often to make sure they don't stick together. Turn down the heat to medium and boil the rivels for 15 minutes.

If using fresh corn, slice the niblets from the cob by holding the cob vertically with the widest (stem) end against the work surface. Using a large, sharp knife, slice from top to bottom all the way around the cob. If using frozen corn, do not defrost before using. Add the corn, parsley, hard-boiled eggs, salt and pepper and chicken back to the stockpot. Continue to simmer until slightly thickened, about 10 minutes. If the soup is too thick, add boxed chicken stock to taste.

Serves 8 to 10

Amish Streuselkuchen
Pennsylvania Dutch Crumb Cake

Mrs Charlene Van Brookhoven, whose family has lived in Pennsylvania Dutch Lancaster County since the American War of Independence, has adopted a number of recipes from her Amish and Mennonite neighbours. This simple crumb or coffee cake is enriched with a good amount of saffron – enough to flavour the cake and to give it a deep yellow hue. You may use more saffron if you like – up to half a teaspoon. Like many of the heritage cooks in her area, she uses locally grown saffron in her recipes, from soups to dessert.

2 cups (400 g) granulated sugar
3 cups (375 g) all-purpose flour
1 tsp cream of tartar
1 tsp baking soda
1 cup (224 g) margarine, or ½ (112 g) cup margarine and ½ (112 g) cup softened butter
1 cup (0.25 l) buttermilk
¼ tsp saffron threads
2 eggs, beaten
1 tsp vanilla

Preheat the oven to 350°F (180°C). Spray or butter three 9-in. round cake pans with baking spray. Whisk together the sugar, flour, cream of tartar and baking soda in a large mixing bowl or the bowl of a stand mixer fitted with a paddle attachment. Add margarine or margarine–butter mix and, using the paddle attachment, mix until crumbly. Alternatively, use a pastry cutter or fork to cut in the butter until the mixture is crumbly. Reserve ½ cup (54 g) of these crumbs for the top of the cakes. Gently heat the buttermilk in a small saucepan until just steaming. Remove from the heat and add the saffron. Allow to cool. Add the saffron, buttermilk, eggs and vanilla to the flour mixture and mix until all the crumbs are moistened and you have a light batter. Pour the batter evenly into the buttered pie pans and sprinkle the crumbs evenly on top. Bake the cakes for 40–45 minutes or until a cake tester inserted into the centre comes out clean.

Makes three 9-in. (23 cm) round cakes

Apricot, Rose and Saffron Bread Pudding

This bread pudding makes use of cardamom, a spice used religiously in Persian desserts, as well as apricot, a beloved Middle Eastern fruit. Aromatic, sweet and slightly tart, this bread pudding combines these traditional flavours. The addition of saffron makes it a more luxurious 'company-worthy' bread pudding with a golden hue that is striking against the whiteness of the whipped cream. Rather than serving this dessert in the free-form dollop that is most usual with bread pudding, I bake it in a loaf pan so I can serve it in slices garnished with the whipped cream that is flavoured with rose-water syrup.

For the bread pudding:
4 cups (340 g) ½-inch bread cubes from stale white bread or brioche bread
2 cups (0.5 l) whole milk
2 tsp unsalted butter
1 cup (175 g) dried apricots, minced
¼ cup (30 g) candied ginger, minced
⅛ tsp sea (kosher) salt
⅛ tsp cardamom powder
½ tsp cinnamon
⅛ tsp nutmeg, preferably freshly grated
¾ cup white sugar
1 tsp vanilla extract
½ tsp ground saffron
2 large eggs

For the whipped cream:
1 cup (0.25 l) heavy (double) cream
¼ cup (30 g) confectioner's (icing) sugar
¼ tsp rose syrup or rose water
1 drop vanilla extract

Place bread cubes in a large bowl. Pour 1 cup of the milk over the bread and mix to coat. Set aside. Heat a large sauté pan over a medium heat and add the butter. When the butter has melted, add the apricot and ginger. Cook, stirring constantly, just until the apricot begins to brown, 2 to 3 minutes. Stir in the salt and remove from heat. Heat the remaining milk with the cardamom, cinnamon and nutmeg in a medium saucepan over a medium-low heat. When the milk begins to steam, whisk in the sugar. Continue to heat until the sugar dissolves, about 2 minutes. Stir in the apricot and ginger. Add the vanilla and saffron. Remove from heat and thoroughly cool. Once the milk mixture is cool, whisk in the eggs until combined. Add the softened bread cubes and toss to thoroughly combine. Set aside for 20 minutes to allow the bread to absorb more liquid. Preheat the oven to 350°F (180°C). Butter or spray with cooking spray a large loaf or terrine pan. Pour the bread mixture into the pan, pushing down gently with a rubber spatula to tightly pack. (Some of the milk may rise to the top of the pan or dish.) Place the pan in a larger baking dish, and place the baking dish in the oven. Pour hot water into the baking dish until it rises about halfway up the side of the loaf pan. Bake until the pudding does not jiggle when shaken and the top crust is golden brown – about 35 minutes. Remove and cool until slightly warm.

While the bread pudding is cooling, make the whipped cream. Place the cream, sugar, rose water extract or syrup and vanilla in the bowl of a stand mixer with whisk attachment. Whip on medium until the whipped cream holds stiff peaks. Alternatively, you may whip the cream by hand with a balloon whisk or using a handheld stand mixer.

Serve the bread pudding. Place a large platter over it. Upturn the baking dish onto the platter. Cut into slices 1- in. (2.5 cm) thick and serve as a dessert with the rose whipped cream. Refrigerate any unused portion of pudding.

Serves 6 to 8

Arancini

Made from cold saffron risotto that is cooled completely, then rolled into small balls, breaded and deep fried, arancini are a delectable appetizer or a meal in themselves. They can be made from leftover saffron risotto in what is possibly one of the best uses of 'repurposed' leftovers around.

2 tbsp olive oil

1 small red onion, minced

½ small carrot, minced

½ stalk celery, minced

½ lb (230 g) pancetta, diced

1 tbsp tomato paste

1 medium shallot, minced

1½ cups (300 g) Arborio rice

¼ tsp saffron powder

¼ cup (25 g) grated parmesan

salt and freshly ground black pepper, to taste

2 eggs

2 cups (220 g) breadcrumbs

1½ cups (375 ml) olive oil, for frying

Heat 1 tablespoon of the olive oil in a large frying pan over a medium heat. Add the onion, carrot and celery, and cook, stirring often, until soft, about 8 to 9 minutes. Add the pancetta and fry until crispy and browned, about 10 minutes. Pour off most of the fat and stir in the tomato paste, reduce heat to medium-low, and cook, stirring occasionally for 5 to 10 minutes. Set aside to cool, then place in a bowl and refrigerate until cold. Heat the second tablespoon of olive oil in a deep, medium saucepan over a medium-high heat. Add the shallot and cook, stirring, until soft, about 2 minutes. Add the rice and stir to coat. Add 1½ cups (375 ml) water and bring to the boil. Stir in the saffron, cover and remove from the heat. Let stand for 20 minutes, then stir in the parmesan, salt and pepper. Spread the rice mixture out on a cookie sheet lined with parchment and allow to cool completely. It will become firm. Beat the eggs in a large, shallow bowl or baking dish and place the breadcrumbs in another large, shallow bowl or dish.

To make the arancini: dampen your hands with cold water. Place 1 heaped tablespoon – about the size of a golf ball – of the rice mixture in the palm of your hand; flatten into a disc. Spoon a teaspoon of the chilled meat filling into the centre of the rice disc and gently pinch the disc closed so that the rice completely covers the filling. Gently press into a ball. Repeat until all the filling and rice is used. Roll each rice ball in the egg mixture and in the breadcrumbs, turning until totally coated. Transfer each ball onto a baking dish or cookie sheet and refrigerate for 30 minutes until firm. Heat a large, heavy-bottomed saucepan over a medium heat and add the oil. Heat until a deep-fry thermometer reads 360°F (182°C) or a pinch of flour dropped into the oil sizzles immediately. Add the rice balls in a single layer, and fry until golden all around. Don't crowd the rice balls into the pan – work in several batches if necessary. Remove with a slotted spoon and place on a wire rack set over a cookie sheet or a tray lined with paper towels. Cool slightly before serving.

Makes about 24

Swedish Saffron Buns (*Lussekatter*)

Saffron does not grow in Sweden, yet it is used in special-occasion dishes such as these pastries, served originally on St Lucia's Day on 13 December, a saint's day with medieval roots. Saffron most likely came to Sweden through trade with other European countries such as Italy or France and, as in other cultures, its high cost would have relegated it to a status ideal for celebratory feasting. Today, *Lussekatter* are eaten throughout the December holiday period and are most often associated with Christmas. Interestingly, the buns are always formed into an S-shape – perhaps in homage to saffron.

¾ cup (175 ml) milk
1 tsp plus ¼ cup (50 g) white, granulated sugar
¾ tsp saffron threads
2¼ tsp packet active dry yeast
3½ cups (490 g to 570 g) all-purpose flour, plus more as needed
½ tsp sea (kosher) salt
¼ tsp cardamom
2 oz (60 g) unsalted butter, softened
¼ cup (60 ml) sour cream
2 large eggs

1 egg, beaten, for egg wash
raisins

Combine the milk, 1 teaspoon of the sugar and the saffron in a small pot over a medium-low heat. Heat until the milk is steamy, 2 to 3 minutes, but do not allow it to come to the boil. Stir well so that the sugar is dissolved. Remove from the heat until the milk temperature reduces to 110–115°F (45°C). Sprinkle the yeast over the milk and set aside until it is bubbly, about 1 to 2 minutes. Whisk together the flour, salt and cardamom in the bowl of a stand mixer then make a well in the middle of the flour. Attach the dough hook to the mixer. Pour in the saffron milk mixture then add the butter, sour cream and the two large eggs. Mix on medium-low speed until all the ingredients are incorporated. Add more flour, 1 tablespoon at a time, until you achieve a smooth, elastic dough that comes away from the sides of the bowl but is still tender to the touch. Remove the dough hook and form the saffron dough into a ball. Cover the bowl with a plastic wrap and set aside to rise in a warm, dry place until it has doubled in size, anywhere from 1 to 2 hours.

Punch down the risen dough and cut it into 12 equal pieces. Roll each piece into a 'snake' about 14 in. (35 cm) long. Form an S-shape by rolling each end of the dough in opposite directions like a roll of tape. Place each shaped bun on a parchment-lined cookie sheet to rise for a second time. Do not crowd the buns on the sheet – allow 1 to 2 in. (2.5–5 cm) all around. Use multiple cookie sheets if necessary. Cover the *Lussekatter* with plastic wrap and allow them to rise for up to an hour or until they double in size.

Preheat oven to 400°F (200°C). Brush each *Lussekatter* with egg wash and place a raisin in the middle of each of the S-spirals. Bake the buns for 10 to 12 minutes or until firm and golden brown. Rotate each cookie sheet halfway through baking to ensure even browning.

Makes 1 dozen buns

Chicken Korma

Chicken Korma is a north Indian dish that is popular on Indian restaurant menus in the West. It can be made with or without saffron, but the addition of saffron provides a deep yellow hue and another level of delicate flavour. As with many Indian saffron-based dishes, chicken korma is popular for special events such as weddings.

1-pint (490 g) plain full fat yoghurt
4 cloves garlic, crushed
2 tbsp grated ginger
3 lb (1.4 kg) boneless, skinless, chicken breast
1 tsp ground saffron
2 tbsp boiling water
6 tbsp coconut oil
2 medium yellow onions, sliced thinly
1 tbsp garam masala
¼ tsp cayenne pepper
1 tsp salt
3 cups (0.75 l) water or chicken stock
¼ cup (65 g) almond butter

In a medium bowl, mix together the yoghurt, garlic and ginger until well combined. Cut each chicken breast into three equal pieces and place in a shallow baking dish. Pour the yoghurt mixture over it, cover in plastic wrap and refrigerate for at least 3 hours, or ideally overnight.

Place the saffron in the boiling water in a small bowl and set aside to cool. Heat the coconut oil in a large, deep saucepan over medium heat. Make sure that the pan is wide enough to accommodate the chicken pieces. Add the onions to the oil and fry until golden brown. Remove the onions from the heat with a slotted spoon and place on a plate lined with paper towels. Add the garam masala to the remaining oil in the pan and fry for 1 minute, then add the chicken pieces and fry for 5 to 6 minutes. When the yoghurt begins to separate, add the cayenne and salt. Pour in the water or chicken stock and mix well. Bring the mixture to a boil and lower to a simmer. Mix in the almond butter and stir well. Simmer uncovered for 25 minutes. Stir in the saffron water and cook for 1 to 2 more minutes. Serve hot with rice.

Serves 6

Classic Seafood Paella

Spain is often credited with having the best saffron, although its production is highly limited and today much Spanish saffron is rebranded from other countries, usually Iran. Saffron makes its way into many classic dishes, including paella. It is important to use the right rice when making paella. Spanish bomba rice, the traditional choice, absorbs more water and has less chance of becoming sticky.

¾ lb (340 g) large shrimp, peeled, deveined and shells reserved
¼ tsp ground saffron
1 dozen littleneck clams, scrubbed
1 dozen mussels, beards removed and scrubbed
2 tbsp extra virgin olive oil
1 small onion, minced
1 medium green pepper, minced
1 medium red pepper, minced
4 cloves garlic, crushed
2 cups (400 g) bomba rice
½ cup (118 ml) dry white, such as Albariño
or Sauvignon Blanc
3 medium tomatoes, seeded and roughly chopped
1 tsp Spanish pimentón (smoked paprika)
1 quart (1 l) chicken stock
salt and freshly ground pepper to taste
2 tbsp freshly minced parsley for garnish
lemon wedges for garnish

Add the shrimp shells to 2½ cups (⅔ l) of water in a medium sauce-pan and simmer for 10 minutes. Strain the broth into a separate bowl and set aside. Dissolve the saffron in ¼ cup (60 ml) of boiling water in a small bowl. Set aside. In a large, deep saucepan, add ½ cup (120 ml) water, the clams and the mussels. Heat on medium-high heat, covered, for 5 to 7 minutes or until the mussels and clams have opened. Remove mussels and clams from pot and set aside. Strain the cooking broth into a clean bowl and set aside. Discard any mussels or clams with unopened shells. Heat a large, wide, deep sauté pan or paella pan over a medium-low heat with olive oil. Add the onion and green and red peppers. Fry for 2 to 3 minutes or until the onion begins to soften, then add the garlic. Stir very well and cook for 1 minute more. Add the bomba rice and stir well to coat, then add the wine, stirring often until the wine is almost totally evaporated. Stir in the tomatoes and mix well. Cook for 1 to 2 minutes. Mix in the pimentón. Add the reserved shrimp stock, reserved clam and mussel broth, and the chicken stock. Stir in the saffron water and mix well. Season with salt and freshly ground pepper to taste, and mix well. Simmer the rice for 10 minutes, stirring once or twice so it is evenly distributed, then add the mussels, clams and raw shrimp to the pan. Cover with a piece of tin foil and turn the heat to low. Cook for 7 to 8 minutes more or until the liquid has been absorbed by the rice but it is slightly firm, or al dente. Serve from the pan garnished with parsley and lemon wedges.

Serves 4 to 6

Kesar Peda

Kesar Peda is a popular Indian *mithai* or dessert that is often served during holy days and celebrations. *Kesar* is the Kashmiri word for saffron. This dessert is usually made with *khoya*, also known as *mawa*, a South Asian milk product, but drained ricotta cheese is a good substitute.

2 tbsp whole milk
½ tsp saffron threads
2 lb (900 g) ricotta cheese
4 tbsp ghee (clarified butter)

2 cups (400 g) sugar
1 cup (128 g) powdered milk
1 tsp ground cardamom
pistachio slivers to garnish

Line a fine mesh sieve with cheesecloth or a clean, cotton dish-cloth that has no nap. Place this over a large bowl. It is ideal if it is suspended over the bowl rather than sitting in it. Scoop the ricotta cheese into the lined sieve, cover with plastic and refrigerate overnight so that the water drains out of the cheese. Heat the milk in a small pan over a low heat for 1 minute (do not allow it to boil) or place in a small microwave-safe bowl and heat for 30 to 40 seconds on high. Remove the milk from the heat and add the saffron threads. Set aside until the milk achieves a deep-orange colour.

Heat the ghee in a large, deep saucepan and add the drained ricotta, sugar and powdered milk. Cook, stirring constantly, until the mixture pulls away from the sides of the pan and comes together in a loose ball at the centre. Add the milk and saffron mixture to the ricotta mixture, along with the cardamom. Mix very well so that the colour is evenly distributed, then set aside to cool. When the mixture is cool, spoon out 1½ to 2 tablespoons (about the size of a ping-pong ball) of the dough and roll into a ball. Slightly flatten the ball with your palms to form a fat disc. Garnish with pistachio slivers.

Makes about 30

Kozani Chicken

On the outskirts of the city of Kozani is Greece's modern-day saffron-growing area; a village called Krokos is most notable for the production of the saffron crocus, which originated in this region. This simple chicken dish melds the astringent and aromatic flavour of saffron with the sweetness of prunes. The dish is traditionally made with bone-in chicken thighs, which give the best flavour, but you may use boneless thighs, too, if you like. Serve with pilau rice or plain white rice.

8 skinless chicken thighs
½ tsp ground saffron
4 tbsp good-quality Greek olive oil
3 red onions, sliced thinly
1 heaped tbsp paprika
1 cup (174 g) pitted prunes
kosher salt and freshly ground black pepper to taste

Place the chicken thighs in a large saucepan with 3 cups (¾ l) water and the saffron over a medium-high heat. Bring to a boil, then reduce the heat to a simmer. Cook for 15 minutes. Remove thighs from the cooking liquid, reserve the liquid. Heat the olive oil in a large sauté pan over a medium heat and add the onions. Fry for 8 to 10 minutes or until the onions are very soft and beginning to lightly brown. Stir in the paprika and cook for another 1 to 2 minutes, then add the chicken thighs, the reserved saffron cooking liquid and prunes. Season with salt and freshly ground black pepper to taste and simmer for another 10 minutes, or until the sauce is reduced by about a third. Serve the chicken and sauce over pilaf rice.

Serves 4

Jalebi

Street vendors in South Asia and in Indian-diasporic communities such as Trinidad in the Caribbean sell this fritter resembling flat curly fries year round. Made from a loose, yeasty dough that crisps ups nicely, it is best eaten when it's freshly made and hot. Jalebi are traditionally doused with sugar syrup flavoured with rose water, but honey works just as well.

1 tsp active dry yeast
2 cups (400 g) sugar
3 cups (710 ml) warm water (100–110°F/40–45°C)
½ tsp ground saffron
¼ cup (60 ml) boiling water

2 cups (250 g) all-purpose flour
1 cup (220 ml) canola (rapeseed) oil, for frying
2 tsp rose-water syrup

Place the yeast in a small bowl and sprinkle with ¼ tsp of the sugar. Add ¼ cup (60 ml) of the warm water and set the yeast mixture aside until it bubbles. Place the ground saffron in a small bowl with the boiling water. Allow to sit for 5 to 10 minutes or until the water becomes a deep orange-yellow. Combine the yeast mixture with the flour. Gradually add 1¾ cups (410 ml) more of warm water until the mixture achieves the consistency of yoghurt. Stir in half the saffron mixture. Set aside overnight in a warm place.

Before making the jalebi, bring 1 cup of water to a simmer with the remaining sugar. Stir in the remaining saffron liquid and simmer until the mixture reaches the consistency of maple syrup, about 5 minutes. Set aside. Pour the jalebi mixture into a squeeze bottle or a pitcher with a narrow spout. Heat the oil in a deep pan. Test the oil by adding a drop of jalebi batter to it. If the batter immediately bubbles and bobs to the top, the oil is hot enough. Squeeze or pour the jalebi dough in overlapping, spiralling circles, about 4 in. (10 cm) in diameter into the hot oil. Fry until golden brown on both sides. Remove and drain on a plate lined with paper towels. Transfer the jalebis to a bowl and pour the syrup evenly over them so all the sides are coated.

Makes about 24 fritters

Persian Halva

I find this dessert irresistible because of the combination of nutty flavours from the toasted flour and the saffron. It is mostly served during funerals or during Ramadan, the Muslim month of fasting, so it is rare to come by it simply as a sweet treat. Intense, deeply orange saffron water is necessary for this dish. The word 'halva' applies to any number of Middle Eastern or South Asian desserts with a paste or soft-butter-like consistency.

½ tsp ground saffron
¼ cup (60 ml) boiling water
1 cup (200 g) sugar
2 cups (0.5 l) water
¼ tsp cardamom
1 tbsp rose water
4 oz (113 g) (1 stick) sweet cream butter
1 cup (125 g) flour
slivered almonds for garnish

In a small bowl, dissolve the saffron in the boiling water and set aside. In a medium saucepan, combine the sugar, water and cardamom. Bring to a boil, then reduce to a simmer over a medium heat. Simmer for 2 to 3 minutes or until slightly thickened. Stir in the rose water and set aside. In a large, deep saucepan, melt the butter over a medium heat and add the flour, stirring continuously until the mixture turns deep golden brown, about 5 to 7 minutes. Pour in the sugar mixture and mix well until combined. Add the saffron mixture and mix well. Continue to cook, stirring constantly until the mixture thickens and comes away from sides of the pan, about 2 to 3 minutes. It should be the consistency of a thick paste. Spoon the halva onto a plate and smooth with the back of a spoon. Garnish with almond slivers and allow to cool before serving.

Serves 4

Persian Saffron Ice Cream (*Bastani Sonnati*)

The ancient Persians were known for making *sharbat*, summertime drinks of fruit juice, sweetened with honey and chilled with mountain snow. It was the Arabs who improvised on the idea to create frozen concoctions more closely related to what we would recognize today as ice cream.

While today one can get virtually any flavour of ice cream in Iran, traditionally ice cream was a saffron-flavoured confection, enhanced with pistachio, rose water and rose petals. Rich with cream and egg yolks, *bastani* is an incredibly decadent dessert that sometimes also contains chunks of pure frozen cream. A little of this Persian ice cream goes a long way.

1 ½ cups (375 ml) heavy (double) cream
1 ½ cups (375 ml) whole milk
¾ cup (150 g) sugar
¼ tsp salt
½ tsp ground saffron
2 tbsp food-grade rose water such as Cortas or Sadaf brands
1 tsp vanilla extract
6 egg yolks
¼ cup (27 g) sliced pistachios
food-grade rose petals for garnish (available in Middle Eastern shops)

Combine the cream, milk, sugar, salt and saffron in a large, deep saucepan over a medium heat. Whisk well and keep whisking until the sugar dissolves, about 2 to 3 minutes. Lower the heat to medium-low, without allowing the mixture to boil, and cook for another 2 to 3 minutes. Stir in the rose water and vanilla and mix well. Remove from the heat. Whisk the egg yolks in a large, heatproof bowl and slowly pour in the hot-milk mixture while whisking vigorously. Continue pouring and whisking until all the milk mixture is used. Return the mixture back to the saucepan. Place the saucepan over a medium-low heat and cook, whisking until the mixture thickens, about 2 to 3 minutes. Strain the mixture through a fine sieve and allow to cool slightly. Cover the ice-cream custard mixture with plastic wrap, placing the wrap right against the top of the mixture, and refrigerate until cold.

Add the pistachio slices to the ice-cream custard and pour the mixture into the bowl of an ice-cream maker. Churn the saffron ice-cream custard in an ice-cream maker following the manufacturer's directions. When the ice cream is hard, scoop into a quart (litre) container and freeze for at least 2 hours. Serve garnished with rose petals.

Makes about 1 quart (1 litre)

Persian Saffron Rice Pudding (*Sholeh Zard*)

Sholeh zard is a special-occasion dessert in Iran and serves multiple cultural purposes. It is often served at dinners to break the fast during the Muslim holy month of Ramadan, as well as during Tirgan, or the summer solstice, one of the four major holidays of the ancient Persian Zoroastrian religion (which are still celebrated in Iran today).

1 tsp ground saffron
1 cup (185 g) basmati rice
¼ tsp coarse salt
2 cups (400 g) sugar
4 tbsp butter
2 tbsp rose water
½ tsp ground cardamom
¾ tsp cinnamon, plus more as desired for garnish
2 tbsp slivered almonds

Dissolve the saffron in ¼ cup of boiling water and set aside. Wash the rice by placing it in a deep bowl and filling the bowl with cold water. Swirl the water around with your hand until it is cloudy. Carefully drain the water. Repeat 4 or 5 times until the water is clear. Set aside. Place the rice in a large deep saucepot with the salt and add just enough water to cover the surface of the rice by ½ inch. Simmer for 15 minutes, stirring once or twice. Add the sugar and cook for another 10 minutes, or until the sugar dissolves. Add the butter, rose water, cardamom and cinnamon and continue to cook until the water is absorbed, and the mixture forms a thick pudding. Remove from the heat and allow to cool to room temperature. Serve garnished with slivered almonds and cinnamon arranged in a pattern of your choice.
Serves 4 to 6

Saffron Beurre Blanc

Beurre blanc is a classic French preparation that is most often served with 'white' proteins such as fish, shellfish, chicken or pork. The trick to beurre blanc is that the butter should be cold. Cream is not strictly necessary, but it does add some 'insurance' that the sauce won't break.

½ cup (120 ml) dry white wine
½ cup (120 ml) white wine vinegar
2 shallots, minced
2 sprigs fresh thyme
¼ cup (60 ml) heavy (double) cream
¼ tsp saffron threads
4 oz (115 g) (1 stick) cold, unsalted butter, cut into 10 pieces
¼ tsp salt
¼ tsp freshly ground pepper

Combine the white wine, wine vinegar, shallots and thyme in a small saucepan over a medium heat. Simmer until the liquid is reduced by three-quarters, about 3 to 5 minutes. Stir in the heavy cream and add the saffron threads. Reduce the heat to low and stir well. Allow to heat until the saffron has coloured the sauce a deep yellow, about 1 minute. Add the butter, 1 piece at a time, whisking after each addition. Repeat until all the butter is used and you have a thick sauce. Season with salt and pepper. Remove thyme sprigs and serve with chicken or fish.
Makes about ½ a cup (118 ml) of sauce

Risotto Milanese

This northern Italian rice dish is known for the deep yellow-orange hue imparted by the saffron. Though simple, it is largely considered the most classic of all risottos. This method produces a rich, creamy risotto using the oven rather than standing over a hot stove, constantly stirring the Arborio rice in the traditional way.

½ tsp ground saffron
2 tbsp boiling water
1 tbsp olive oil
1 large shallot, minced
1 cup (200 g) Arborio rice
salt and pepper to taste
¼ cup (60 ml) dry white wine
1 quart (1 l) chicken stock
1 cup (180 g) finely grated Parmesan cheese

Preheat oven to 350°F (180°C).

Dissolve the saffron in the boiling water and allow to steep until cool. Heat a heavy-bottomed 2-quart (2 l) saucepan over a medium heat and add the olive oil. Add the shallot and fry for 1 minute, then add the Arborio rice. Mix well until the rice is well coated. Add the salt and pepper and the white wine. Mix until the wine is evaporated. Mix in the chicken stock and the saffron liquid, and cover with a heatproof lid. Place in the oven for 20 to 25 minutes. Remove from the oven, add the Parmesan cheese and mix vigorously with a wooden spoon. Serve hot.
Serves 4

Saffron Sweet Milk (Kesari Sweet Milk)

This dessert-like drink features almonds, cardamom and saffron – a classic combination in Middle Eastern and northern Indian sweets. Food-grade rose petals for the garnish can be found in Middle Eastern grocery stores.

⅓ cup (35 g) slivered almonds
4 cups (1 l) whole milk
¼ tsp saffron threads
¼ cup (50 g) sugar
½ tsp cardamom powder
slivered pistachios for garnish
food-grade rose petals for garnish

Combine the almonds and 3 tbsp of the milk in a high-powered blender, and process to a smooth paste, adding more milk as necessary. Set aside. Combine the remaining milk and saffron in a medium saucepan over a low heat for 3 to 5 minutes, or until the saffron releases a deep-orange colour throughout the milk. Do not allow the milk to boil. Add the almond paste mixture, sugar and cardamom to the milk mixture and raise the heat to medium-low. Cook, stirring until all the sugar dissolves. Do not allow the milk to boil. Serve warm or cold, garnished with slivered pistachios and rose petals.

Serves 4 to 6

References

1 Flower of the Gods: Origin and Early Cultivation

1 'Gli amori poi de Croco, e di Smilace, che furono ambidoi conversi in fiori, non havendo potuto godersi insieme . . .', Giovanni Andrea dell'Anguillara, trans., *Le metamorfosi di Ovidio . . . con le annotationi di M. Gioseppe Horologgi & gli argomenti & pastille di M. Farncesco Turchi*, rev. edn (Venice, 1584), p. 152.

2 Z. Nemati et al., 'Saffron (*Crocus sativus*) Is an Autotriploid that Evolved in Attica (Greece) from Wild *Crocus cartwrightianus*', *Molecular Phylogenetics and Evolution*, cxxxvi (2019), pp. 14–20.

3 J. Timbs, *Things Not Generally Known, Familiarly Explained: A Book for Old and Young* (London, 1866) p. 132.

4 J. Spurrier, *The Practical Farmer; being a New and Compendious System of Husbandry, Adapted to the Different Soils and Climate of America* (Wilmington, DE, 1793), p. 349, available at https://quod.lib.umich.edu.

5 Rachel Dewan, 'Bronze Age Flower Power: The Minoan Use and Social Significance of Saffron and Crocus Flowers', *Chronika*, 5 (2015), pp. 42–55.

6 Interview with Martin Keen by Ramin Ganeshram in May 2018.

2 The Ancient World and the Silk Road

1 Pat Willard, *Secrets of Saffron: The Vagabond Life of the World's Most Seductive Spice* (Boston, MA, 2001), pp. 19–20.
2 Herodotus, 'The Persian Wars', Book 8, Paragraph 98, www.parstimes.com.
3 A. Dalby, *Dangerous Tastes: The Story of Spices* (Berkeley, CA, 2002), p. 95.

3 Saffron in the Medieval and Renaissance Eras

1 Mohammad J. Siddiqui et al., 'Saffron (*Crocus sativus* L.): As an Antidepressant', *Journal of Pharmacy and Bioallied Sciences*, X/4 (2018), pp. 173–80.
2 Behjat Javadi et al., 'A Survey on Saffron in Major Islamic Traditional Medicine Books', *Iranian Journal of Basic Medical Sciences*, XVI/1 (2013), pp. 1–11.
3 Columella, *De rustica*, Loeb Classical Library edition, p. 277, http://penelope.uchicago.edu.
4 R. Hakluyt, *Principle Navigations, Voyages, Traffics and Discoveries of the English Nation* (London, 1598).
5 Wolfgang von Stromer, 'Nuremberg in the International Economics of the Middle Ages', *Business History Review*, XLIV/2 (1970), pp. 210–25.
6 Volker Schier, 'Probing the Mystery of the Use of Saffron in Medieval Nunneries', *The Senses and Society*, V/1 (2015), pp. 57–72.

4 North America and the Caribbean

1 Martha Washington, *Martha Washington's Book of Cookery* (New York, 1981), p. 398.

5 Arts and Medicine

1 A. Ferdowsi, *Shahnameh: The Persian Book of Kings*, trans. D. Davis (New York, 2006), p. 131.

2 J. Mandeville, *The Travels of Sir John Mandeville* (New York, 1923), Chapter 27.

3 A. Dalby, *Dangerous Tastes: The Story of Spices* (Berkeley, CA, 2002), p. 95.

4 Mandana Barkeshli and H. Ataie, 'pH Stability of Saffron Used in Verdigris as an Inhibitor in Persian Miniature Paintings', *Restaurator*, XXIII/3 (2002), pp. 154–64.

5 Metropolitan Museum of Art, New York, 'Bangali Ragini: Folio from a Ragamala Series (Garland of Musical Modes)' [1709] www.metmuseum.org, accessed 1 February 2020.

6 A. Hosseini, B. M. Razavi and H. Hosseinzadeh, 'Saffron (*Crocus sativus*) Petal as a New Pharmacological Target: A Review', *Iran Journal of Basic Medical Science*, XXI/11 (2018), pp. 1091–9.

7 Hossein Hosseinzadeh, 'Saffron: A Herbal Medicine of Third Millennium', *Jundishapur Journal of Natural Pharmaceutical Products*, IX/1 (2014), pp. 1–2.

8 Ibid.

9 Ibid.

10 John D. Kakisis, 'Saffron: From Greek Mythology to Contemporary Anti-atherosclerotic Medicine', *Atherosclerosis*, CCLXVIII (2018), pp. 193–5.

6 The Modern Market

1 Hans Rotteveel, 'Saffron: It's Beautiful, Tasty and Expensive', www.uvm.edu/~saffron, accessed 10 March 2020.

2 Marco Polo, *Travels of Marco Polo*, intro. John Masefield (New York, 1908), p. 314.

3 John Beckman, *A History of Inventions and Discoveries*, trans. William Johnston (London, 1814), vol. 1, p. 180.

4 *A Saffron Tablet Market: Global Industry Analysis, Size, Share, Growth, Trends and Forecast, 2017–2025* (Market Research Reports), https://amazingherald.com, accessed 30 June 2019.

Select Bibliography

Dewan, Rachel, 'Bronze Age Flower Power: The Minoan Use
    and Social Significance of Saffron and Crocus Flowers',
    Chronika, 5 (2015), pp. 42–55
Gerard, John, *The Herball, or, Generall Historie of Plantes. Gathered
    by John Gerarde of London, Master in Chirurgerie* (London, 1597)
Hess, Karen, *Martha Washington's Booke of Cookery* (New York,
    1981)
Humphries, John, *The Essential Saffron Companion* (Berkeley,
    CA, 1998)
Srivastava, R., et al., '*Crocus sativus L.*: A Comprehensive Review',
    Pharmacognosy Reviews, IV/8 (2010), pp. 200–208
Willard, Pat, *Secrets of Saffron: The Vagabond Life of the World's
    Most Seductive Spice* (Boston, MA, 2001)

Websites and Associations

University of Vermont, North American Center
for Saffron Research and Development
www.uvm.edu/~saffron/

Saffron Instiute (India)
http://saffroninstitute.in

United Nations Food & Agriculture Organization, Saffron
Global Heritage Sites
www.fao.org

Saffron Recipes

Saffron Recipes that Make Most of Precious Spice
(*Saveur Magazine*)
www.saveur.com

10 Golden Recipes for your Fancy Saffron (Food Republic)
www.foodrepublic.com

Get the Most from a Pinch of Saffron (*Fine Cooking*)
www.finecooking.com

Acknowledgements

When I set out to write a book about saffron, I didn't fully realize the passion that this legendary ingredient sparks in the hearts of those who love it. As a person of Iranian descent, saffron was just a part of life – a *necessary* part of life, certainly, but not one which, to my mind, would elicit such passion.

In the course of writing this book, I rarely met anyone with a lukewarm reaction to saffron. It was rare even to find anyone who claimed to dislike it; although I did meet a few, they were the rare exception. More often than not, those who were not avowed saffron lovers tended to be ignorant of the spice, other than having a passing knowledge. That knowledge was mostly with respect to how costly the spice was and how difficult to procure.

The most fascinating aspect of researching this work was learning about the twenty-first-century efforts to grow saffron beyond its traditional cultivation areas. I realized the efforts of these intrepid farmers, most of whom have no deep cultural affiliation with the saffron crocus, are not only impressive but key to maintaining the allure and value of saffron as the undisputed queen of spices. I am grateful to all these new saffron farmers whose dedication serves to remind me how precious saffron is to those of us who have been blessed to grow up with it in our families' culinary traditions.

I owe a debt of gratitude to those dedicated saffron-lovers – growers, cultivators, chefs and home cooks – who shared their stories, knowledge and recipes with me in order to write this book.

They include Charlene Van Brookhoven and Martin Keen from Lancaster County, PA, chef Vikas Khanna, food writer Monica Bhide and those in my own family whose recipes and knowledge about handling saffron to get the best colour, aroma and flavour have been handed down through the generations.

Working with these saffron aficionados was, in many ways, the next best thing to having a time machine. Their experiences of the struggles and triumphs of procuring, growing and using saffron correspond so closely to what the historical texts described centuries ago that it is easy to understand why saffron maintains its supremacy as the queen of spices.

Photo Acknowledgements

The author and publishers wish to express their thanks to the below sources of illustrative material and/or permission to reproduce it. Some locations of artworks are also given below, in the interest of brevity:

Photo Alice Alphabet/Pixabay: p. 96; from *Arzneibuch* (Austria or South Germany, *c.* 1675), photo courtesy Wellcome Library, London (MS990): p. 52; photo Jonas Bergsten: p. 51; from Giorgio Bonelli, *Hortus romanus secundum systema J. P. Tournefortii . . .*, vol. VI (Rome, 1780), courtesy The New York Public Library: p. 53; British Museum, London: p. 71; photo Bogdan Ch/Pixabay: p. 6; photos Ramin Ganeshram: pp. 12, 13; Gemäldegalerie Alte Meister, Dresden: p. 18; from Johann Ferdinand Hertodt, *Crocologia seu Curiosa Croci Regis Vegetabilium Enucleatio* (Jena, 1671): p. 54; Historic New England, Boston: p. 60; hlphoto/Shutterstock: p. 10; from *The Illustrated History of the World, for the English People*, vol. 1 (London, 1881), courtesy Robarts Library, University of Toronto: p. 32; Philippe Imbault/Shutterstock: p. 81; Indian Food Images/Shutterstock: p. 66; photo Vikas Khanna: p. 19; Kulnisha Studio/Shutterstock: p. 88; Kuvona/Shutterstock: p. 92; from Sir Austen Henry Layard, *A Second Series of the Monuments of Nineveh* (London, 1853), courtesy The New York Public Library: p. 35; from Prince Louis I of Anhalt-Köthen, *Der Fruchtbringenden Geselschaft Nahmen, Vorhaben, Gemählde und Wörter* (Frankfurt, 1646), courtesy University of Illinois at Urbana-Champaign: p. 75; from George Maw, *A Monograph of the*

Readers are free to:

> share – copy and redistribute the material in any medium or format.
>
> adapt – remix, transform, and build upon the material for any purpose, even commercially.

Under the following terms:

> attribution – You must give appropriate credit, provide a link to the license, and indicate if changes were made. You may do so in any reasonable manner, but not in any way that suggests the licensor endorses you or your use.
>
> share alike – If you remix, transform, or build upon the material, you must distribute your contributions under the same license as the original.

Index

italic numbers refer to illustrations; **bold** to recipes